Stretch without breaking—every good leader lives in that tension, and makes sure followers do too. Nancy Ortberg's combination of practical experience and communication skills makes her a leader worth listening to. This book is not just moving—it will help you move your team to a higher level.

BILL HYBELS • senior pastor, Willow Creek Community Church; chairman of the board, Willow Creek Association

If you are looking for a book that will guide you in polishing your leadership instincts and skills, you have found it. Nancy Ortberg has given us an exciting and authentic look at right leadership.

MAX DePREE • chairman emeritus of Herman Miller, Inc.; author of *Leadership Jazz*

Good leaders get results. Great leaders get results and develop people. Nancy Ortberg is a great leader. She gets it! She knows what it takes to get something done while doing something great in people. *Unleashing the Power of Rubber Bands* is an authentic, practical, and compelling look at what it takes to do that with excellence. If you lead people, ignore this book at your own risk . . . or theirs.

JIM MELLADO • president, Willow Creek Association

This book is a must-read for anyone who wants to become a better leader!

KEN BLANCHARD • coauthor of *The One Minute Manager*

Rarely do I read a book on leadership that leaves me feeling more free and lighthearted than when I started reading. With her non-linear approach (don't go looking for ten steps to anything), delightful humor, and refreshing honesty, Nancy Ortberg writes the same way she lives her life. This is a leadership book for people wired like me, who wonder if we can ever fit a profile of the "typical leader." Thank you, Nancy, for this highly practical, engaging, and totally fun book.

NANCY BEACH • teaching pastor, Willow Creek Community Church; author of *Gifted to Lead: The Art of Leading as a Woman in the Church*

A refreshing and delightful departure from the top-down, out-of-touch drivel of management books. Rubber bands are in and T-shirts are out—read the book to find out why.

GUY KAWASAKI • cofounder of alltop.com, author of *The Art of the Start*

Nancy gives each of us hope that maybe God can use our lives and our leadership, no matter how messy it might look, to make a real difference in this world.

GREG HAWKINS • executive pastor, Willow Creek Community Church; author of *REVEAL: Where Are You?*

unleashing the power of rubber bands

TYNDALE HOUSE PUBLISHERS, INC.
Carol Stream, Illinois

unleashing the
POWER
of rubber bands

lessons in non-linear leadership

NANCY
ORTBERG

Visit Tyndale's exciting Web site at www.tyndale.com

TYNDALE and Tyndale's quill logo are registered trademarks of Tyndale House Publishers, Inc.

Unleashing the Power of Rubber Bands: Lessons in Non-Linear Leadership

Designed by Jennifer Ghionzoli

All Scripture quotations, unless otherwise indicated, are taken from the HOLY BIBLE, NEW INTERNATIONAL VERSION®. NIV®. Copyright © 1973, 1978, 1984 by International Bible Society. Used by permission of Zondervan. All rights reserved.

Library of Congress Cataloging-in-Publication Data

Ortberg, Nancy.
   Unleashing the power of rubber bands : lessons in non-linear leadership / Nancy Ortberg.
      p. cm.
   ISBN-13: 978-1-4143-2164-6 (hc)
   ISBN-10: 1-4143-2164-3 (hc)
1. Leadership—Religious aspects—Christianity.   I. Title.
   BV4597.53.L43O78 2008
   253—dc22   2008009924

Printed in the United States of America

14   13   12   11   10   09   08
7   6   5   4   3   2   1

TO JAMIE BARR,

who told me, when I was nineteen years old, that I was a leader . . .

and then made sure I lived up to all that meant

CONTENTS

Foreword

The world is full of advice, much of it wonderful, about how to be a better person or parent or leader. Sifting through it all and deciding what warrants your time and energy is a nontrivial challenge. Nancy Ortberg makes that challenge easier here because of her unique insights, effortless storytelling ability, and genuine humility and self-deprecation.

Nancy is a person who walks through life with both eyes wide open, taking in everything available to her and searching for meaning and connection. In *Unleashing the Power of Rubber Bands*, she provides her readers with thoughtful advice and disarmingly selfless perspective on everything from personal development and empathy to innovation and teamwork. And she does it with a deep sense of the fundamental place God has in it all.

Like Nancy herself, this book will be hard for readers to peg, as it rolls around and touches upon so many topics that are seemingly diverse but inextricably linked. And because it is as inspiring as it is practical, you may find it difficult to decide whether to take it to work, keep it on your nightstand, or tuck it away into a suitcase. Whatever you do, keep it handy for those times when you find yourself with a few spare minutes that just might transform your life.

Patrick Lencioni
Author of *The Five Dysfunctions of a Team*
President, The Table Group

Author's Note

Very early in my career I learned that my understanding of people would rival my job competencies in determining my leadership success. There have been a number of places where I have been fortunate enough to have been given roles in which to learn that.

For ten years I worked as a registered nurse, in such varied fields as medical-surgical, the emergency department, and home health. I was, for approximately nine years, on staff at Willow Creek Community Church, in roles of teaching pastor and leader of a strengths-based ministry as well as the post-modern expression of the church, called Axis.

Finally, the last few years I have been a consulting partner of Patrick Lencioni with my own leadership consulting firm, Teamworx2, and partners David, Kent, Rick, and Linda.

The common thread in these varied fields has been leadership . . . and this book is a consolidation of what I have learned, through success and failure, as well as what I deeply believe to be true of great leadership.

One of my kids always used to read the last chapter in a book first (and probably still does). That's what I would recommend you do with this book: Read "Understatement of the Year," and that should help you decide if what is in the other chapters is what you are looking for.

Introduction

I love great leadership. I love it when I'm able to observe it, love it when I'm the recipient of it, love it when I'm able to do it. Great leadership takes my breath away, and I have seen it in some of the most surprising places.

It is often spotlighted in large corporations, but I have seen it in a rural McDonald's, a library, a veterinary office, and a small church. I've seen it in a waitress, a salesclerk, and a bus driver. I've seen it in an accounting group, a public high school, and a nursing home. I've even seen it at the DMV, but only once.

Great leadership is occurring in the hands of quiet and unnoticed people who are creating environments where people can bring the best of what they do to what they do best. But you will never see these inspiring leaders on the cover of a magazine or in the six o'clock news.

We greatly underestimate where great leadership is to be found and what we can learn from it. If we only expect to find it in the hands of those select few in positions of obvious power, we are poorer for having overlooked the beauty and strength that's to be found in unexpected places.

Most leaders want to lead in strong and admirable ways, even if what they lead is never the biggest or the best. And most leaders who do it well find ways to develop strong leadership at every level in the organization. They know how to unleash the power that is already in the organization and how to fan the flame of that power in productive and transformational ways.

My hope is that in this book you will find a simplicity and practicality that inspires hope, and come away with a sense that *you* can do leadership better as a result. And by practicality, I don't always mean a clear, step-by-step plan. While that is important, I believe that if plans precede the "why," they nearly always result in less-than-optimal performance. I hope that this book provokes, stimulates, irritates, and ignites you to better leadership. Great leadership is much more about creating a culture, and cultures transform people in much more profound ways than systems do. Systems and processes should always support the vision, but they should never *be* the vision. When you spend time plumbing the depths of "why," you will then be free to formulate the "how," and you will see that there are many great ways to tackle that "how."

I also want to show how closely leadership is tied to both character and to God, because I think the leader ought to be the most transformed person in the organization. A leader works with everyone, sets the tone for an organization, and creates a culture in the office. If you are reading this book and are not a Christ-follower, I guess you could just substitute "higher power" for God, but I would invite you at least once or twice to consider how deeply great leadership is tied to the nature of God.

Much of what gets done in leadership has a strikingly non-linear approach. There is no clear-cut, step-by-step equation that guarantees results; it's the convergence of conditions that creates a climate where people and organizations prosper. I'm guessing since you opened this book after reading the title, you are not looking for a book that presents a linear approach to leadership. But just in case that *is* what you are looking for, I recommend you put this one down and keep looking.

I have read many linear books on leadership, some of which have been enormously helpful. This book is not one of those linear books. Some of my best friends think in that sequential, ordered way, and do great leadership from that perspective. I have even hired, worked with, and benefited greatly from them.

But that is not how my mind works.

Which brings me to the Post-it note.

The first year I led Axis, I was sitting at my desk one morning before the rest of my staff arrived and the meetings and flurry of activities began. On the corkboard that hung above my desk were pictures of my kids, a copy of our vision statement, a strategy spreadsheet (created by some of the aforementioned friends), and a postcard of Bora-Bora.

I really liked our vision statement, and our strategy was well thought out. I had little doubt that if we continued to pray and execute against the strategy, we would make significant progress toward the vision. Everything in the previous sentence is just what a leader is looking for. But for me, something was missing. Turns out it was just a word, but a word that encompassed everything.

So I pulled out a Post-it and wrote the word *Flourish*. Then I stuck that Post-it up on my corkboard, where it stayed for the next five years. Perhaps it was my own personal vision statement—or vision word, I guess. But whenever I looked at that word, I knew what to do.

I guess we all need different things. Some people need a spreadsheet or a detailed plan to know what to do. I needed a word. That word, hung where I could see it every day, went with me in my heart and head and spirit into each meeting, each interaction with people, each conversation I had with myself.

It motivated me to lead well, to build a culture where people and programs and systems could flourish. For me, *flourish* is a very powerful, visceral, and prompting word.

We all have certain conditions under which we flourish.

The coastal hills near our house are lush green right now, bursting with the color of wildflowers. They are so beautiful that driving is dangerous: You can barely take your eyes off of them. The perfect combination of spring rain and sunshine has created this spectacular sight.

There is no exact equation for these conditions, no spreadsheet that monitors and quantifies the correct mixture of rain and sun. People and organizations are no different. Given certain cultural climates, they will grow and accomplish and learn and flourish.

Which leads me to the rubber bands . . .

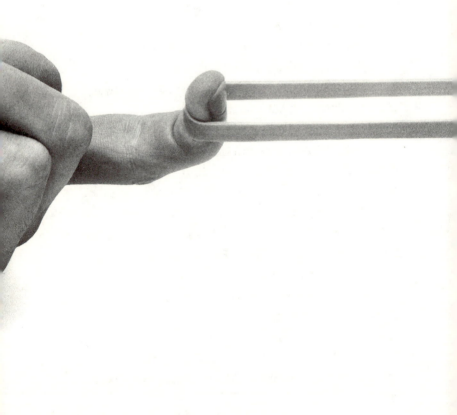

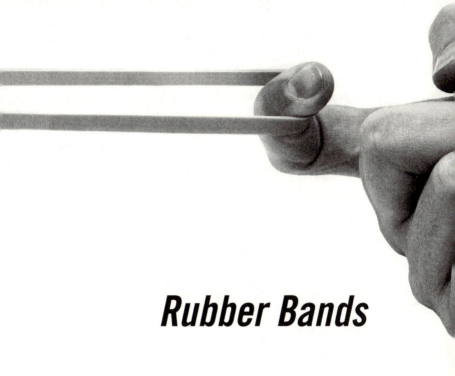

Rubber Bands

AT ITS HEART, LEADERSHIP is about promises, and of all its promises, development is one of the most significant. Sometimes in our attempts to take this seriously, we put together very cumbersome developmental plans. Perhaps it's better than the popular alternative of completely ignoring the issue, but I wonder if we make it too complicated.

One day I was in a meeting of senior leaders at Willow Creek, and Greg Hawkins was talking very excitedly. Which, come to think of it, is the only way I have ever heard Greg talk. . . . Anyway, he was talking about this topic of development and he pulled a thick rubber band out of his pocket. He stretched it between his two hands

1

and said, "Very simply"—Greg is a genius when it comes to making complex issues simple and, therefore, doable—"this is development."

He showed what happened when he moved his hands too far away from each other: The rubber band became taut and clearly in danger of breaking. Stretched too far for too long, the rubber band is ruined.

Then he moved his hands closer together until the rubber band became slack, not at all capable of doing what we hire rubber bands to do. Completely incapable of acting like a decent rubber band.

> Inherent in the leadership relationship is the expectation that over time, the direction you give will result in progress toward maturity, growth in skills and character, and even an increase in your own leadership competencies.

Inherent in the leadership relationship is the expectation that over time, the direction you give will result in progress toward maturity, growth in skills and character, and even an increase in your own leadership competencies.

I think it is a helpful and good discipline to write out a simple developmental plan for the people you lead. And once that plan is written, the best way to implement it is to think of those people as rubber bands. When I was nineteen years old, I'm pretty sure Jamie Barr thought a lot about rubber bands when he thought about me.

Jamie was the high school pastor at my church in Whittier, California. He had spent years as a researcher at the City of Hope National Medical Center before he heard the whisper of the Holy Spirit calling him to seminary. With a heart for high school kids, he eventually landed in the role of youth pastor at the church I was attending. I was a freshman at a nearby college that required a certain number of ministry hours a month, and Jamie's area seemed as good as any.

Over the next five years, Jamie Barr became the first developmental leader in my life. He stretched me and challenged me, he supported and encouraged me, he believed in me and gave me things to do—things that mattered.

Jamie was the first person who ever uttered the words *Nancy, leader,* and *teacher* in the same sentence. Do you understand the power of naming someone's giftedness? The moment and memory of that has propelled me down some of the most significant paths in my life. Those words meant so much because they came from a leader who was stretching me and taking me places for which I had no map.

My most vivid recollections of those years with Jamie include conversations we had directly following either a success or a failure. After I had done something well, he would tell me about it. He would replay the details of what I had done, share his observations regarding it, and talk about the impact my actions had had on the high school kids. Then he would always say something like, "Okay, now get over it"—just in case I was tempted to linger a bit too long in the glory of the win. He kept my head on straight with that comment. I was nineteen, and if someone isn't helping you keep your head on straight at that age, there isn't much hope.

Whenever I did something that didn't fit into the "success" category—when my teaching didn't "click" or I was too glib (I think that only happened once. I am tempted to include one of those smiley faces here, but I don't like them.), or when I made a poor decision or did something that was in my own best interest rather than that of the kids, Jamie would say something like, "So if you had that to do over again, what would you do differently?"

How graciously directive! I wasn't going to get a chance to do it over again, but I *was* going to have a chance to learn from my mistakes and grow enough so that when the next opportunity came I might make a better choice.

So much hope was implied in that tiny question, and the way he worded it helped me to save face a bit. It spared me the crushing things that *could* have been said: "You idiot! How could you possibly do something *that* stupid?"

And believe me, there were times when that would have been the best response. It also spared me from the painful illusions that I didn't need improvement or that problems should be avoided. And it built within me a foundation of strength for the times when I would fail again.

Jamie gave me hope because he intimated that there would be a next time; this mistake, while still a mistake, had not rendered me completely unqualified for another chance.

There was hope in the fact that it was a collaborative question. Jamie allowed me to engage in a conversation about what I could learn and how I could be shaped by that learning. The very best development that a leader can offer engages someone else in the dialogue of learning.

> **The very best development that a leader can offer engages someone else in the dialogue of learning.**

And so Jamie Barr grew me up. As a leader, as a teacher, as a follower of Christ. He gave me opportunities, challenges, and a relationship—three things that form a powerful crucible of development. He stretched me sometimes to the point of pain, but never to the point of breaking. He cared for me genuinely, of that I was never in doubt.

And while I never once saw him take out a written plan, I think Jamie may have had rubber bands on his mind.

the core of *Leadership*

WHATEVER IS AT THE CENTER of something has a lot to do with its quality, whether it is fruit, golf balls, or leadership.

I think the core of leadership is hope.

Leadership is the hope that we can change the things that need to be changed and create what we cannot now imagine. Hope gives us the courage to move forward, the power to forgive, and the grace to keep the promises we have made.

Hope dispels fears. Hope readies us for round two. Hope holds our heads above water and gives us permission to regroup when we are tired. Hope redeems mistakes and prompts the optimism and resilience of a leader.

To lead well, we must possess the strong belief that our best days are ahead of us, always ahead of us. Hope and leadership are inexorably linked.

It is critical for leaders to do whatever they can to stay connected to hope, and to drink deeply from its well. We need to find ways to live that renew the life of God in us because the life of God is a life of hope, a meal that sustains.

Hope and leadership are inexorably linked.

Whenever I experience that wonderful convergence of my efforts and God's gifts, the level of hope within me rises to new levels. Whenever I experience the true nature of God—not the myths of Him to which I sometimes cling like a child clings to a favorite blanket—I am surrounded by a hope that swirls around me in Dolby Stereo.

Hope is like a bone marrow transplant: It changes everything. It invades and permeates. It releases us from cynicism and doubt, and restores belief. And it is stronger than the fear that prompted us to go looking for it in the first place.

Hope breeds confidence.

Hope is contagious.

Recently I met with a young kid. I can call him that because Jake is in his midtwenties and I am not. I could call him some other things as well, because over breakfast he mentioned someone who is in his late forties and referred to him as "an older person." Since late forties is younger than I am, this kid almost wound up getting stuck with the check. But when I was his age, I thought late forties was old, too. Anyway . . .

Jake is finishing up his last year at Stanford business school and has started a 501(c)(3) called Nuru International, which creates innovative, sustainable solutions to extreme poverty. In Swahili, *nuru* means "a small light in the darkness." Jake is a Christ-follower, and he is humble and passionate and gifted to lead this enterprise. Nuru is not a Christian organization per se, but it is led by a handful of committed disciples of Jesus, as well as a few others who have different or no faith background.

This was our second or third meeting, and Jake was taking me through his business model, including his vision, an analysis of the challenges, and the first steps of the plan. He listed out the team formation and the area in Kenya where their pilot project would be taking place. As I listened to his strategy, talked with him about God's unexpected direction, and considered the well-thought-out plans put together by gifted minds of God's people, I felt so hopeful.

With all the key ingredients in place—great thought and planning, visits to the area, meetings with local leadership, the caliber of people and expertise on the team—it seemed quite possible that this could be a stunning and sustainable model for making a dent in extreme poverty. Jake and his team had chosen to focus on the areas of health care, education, agriculture, water/sanitation, and small business development. The group had created a holistic model designed to stir an integrated momentum into action that could, I believed, have enormous implications. There had been, of course, a local leadership development and succession strategy in place right from the beginning.

Then we talked about Jake's financial model and fundraising and partnership opportunities. At the time, the group was about a week away from its first dinner with possible donors. Jake said, "I just hate to ask for favors."

I completely understand that feeling; it makes sense. On one level. But in reality, Jake wasn't going to be asking anyone for any favors.

Jake was going to offer hope. And offer people a chance to be a part of that. His gifts and his passion and his God had converged, and in Jake's heart and mind Nuru had sprung.

Nuru has the potential to relieve the intolerable burden of poverty from people whose names we do not yet know. It has the positioning to allow dependent communities to grow into self-sustaining areas.

Jake is dedicated, committed, thoughtful, thorough, collaborative, and smart. He has done his homework, devised plans and strategies that empower, and integrated standardized and rigorous measurements for his own accountability. He has prayed and listened to God. He has made himself a humble student of other methodologies and sought out experts in his target development areas.

Hope is hard work.

No, Jake would not be asking anyone for a favor; he would extend hope and invite others to join him. We should be the ones thanking him.

Hope has so much power in it. When we release hope in individuals and organizations, they flourish. As leaders, we so **Hope is hard work.** often become overly preoccupied with the wrong things. Things that in and of themselves are good and necessary, but not if we major on them. Few leaders I know have taken seriously the power of hope and done whatever they can to infuse it into their people.

I'm not talking about mindless, inauthentic, cheerleading hope. Real hope is a potent force, and when it sits in the center of things, it becomes an epicenter.

There is a man in our church named Art Flegel. Art was a business leader in the community, serving for years as president of a chain of upscale furniture stores. He is now ninety years old.

Too often, I think, we unfairly stereotype the elderly. We accuse them of being resistant to change and stuck in the old ways of doing things. But here's what I think. I think people who resist change and hold on to the old ways when they are in their twenties become people who resist change and hold on to old ways when they are older. People who embrace change and gravitate toward new ideas in their twenties become people who embrace change and gravitate toward new ideas when they are older.

> **Real hope is a potent force, and when it sits in the center of things, it becomes an epicenter.**

May I present Art Flegel?

Did I mention that he is ninety years old?

Art and his wife, Cleo, live across the street from us, so we get a front-row seat to the way they live. I have decided that I want to be Art Flegel when I grow up. Art always has a sparkle in his eye and a spring in his step. Often at six in the morning when I am stumbling out of our front door in my green robe to try to find the newspaper, I encounter Art. He is in his workout clothes starting his morning walk. And he is in a great mood. I slink back into my house, newspaper in hand, a bit humiliated that I

have been outdone by a ninety-year-old before I have had
my breakfast.

Art is working on a book about his family's geneal-
ogy, and he tends to a front and a backyard that look like
they belong on the cover of *Sunset* magazine. The azaleas,
roses, begonias, and agapanthus are testimony to his green
thumb and his perseverance. He often shows up at our
front door with a handful of breathtaking flowers to grace
our family room.

On the afternoon of Art's ninetieth birthday, John and
I walked over with a cake to help him celebrate. We left
about forty minutes later, shaking our heads. We had both
seen a living example of how we want to grow old. Art
had beamed as he talked about the future—gotta love the
sheer hope in that!

There have been a lot of changes going on in our one-
hundred-and-fifty-year-old church, and Art couldn't stop
talking about them. He said he didn't know how much
longer the Lord would give him, but he sure hoped he
would be around for the next few years to see how the
multisite church campuses were going, especially in reaching people who don't know Christ.

There is a marvelous passage in Psalm 92:12, where the
writer says that the righteous will flourish. I do love that
word for the picture it paints. *Flourish* can look different

in different people, but it is unmistakable when someone is flourishing.

Psalm 92:14 goes on to say this:

> *They will still bear fruit in old age,*
> *they will stay fresh and green.*

That is a great picture of what it might mean to grow old well with God. It is also a great picture of Art Flegel, someone all leaders can aspire to be like.

If it is possible to continue to be productive in old age in a way that is reflected in the phrase "fresh and green," then we would do well as leaders to include people of older generations in our leadership circles. A life lived well with God over the years produces wisdom and hope—such a necessary duo. We would do well to identify the Art Flegels and put them into the game. We would also do well to grow old well with God.

Hope can be released in small ways, like seeds that take root unseen and later reveal their growth.

Hope can be released in small ways, like seeds that take root unseen and later reveal their growth. These small things made such a difference when I started doing more speaking and leading. There were two people in my life who were responsible for giving me those opportunities, and as they did, they also gave me something else that I'll never forget. I'm not even sure these guys were aware of it, but their actions filled me with hope and, therefore, perseverance. Each time they scheduled me to do something, they also scheduled the "next time." So each time I tried something new, I never felt as if my future and all of its opportunities were dependent on the way I handled this one assignment. The message this sent to me, however subliminal, was that I would always get more chances.

The weight of one mistake didn't feel like it was the end; instead, it felt like more of a learning opportunity. I knew that someone was developing me rather than auditioning me. This took so much pressure off and allowed me to do a better job. Of course, I understood that this was not an open-ended invitation to do poorly. I think those who were leading me had made enough observations about my gifts that they were ready to give me chances to develop. And their confidence, communicated to me in multiple opportunities, was strengthening.

Sometimes the gift of hope is about believing in others before they can even see it themselves. I would bet that every leader could point to a number of people who have given him or her that gift along the way.

Another small seed, more team-oriented than individual, is the "autopsy." You wouldn't expect that a word like *autopsy* could contain hope, but I think it does. Healthy teams do autopsies after most of their activities, gathering together both to celebrate and to analyze what happened. Autopsies allow teams to have honest conversations about missing the mark and what they could have done differently or better. While at first glance, this may seem like something difficult that you'd want to avoid, autopsies are actually just the opposite.

Honesty has a way of making things stronger over time.

Too often, we have conversations that are designed to "protect" by ignoring mistakes. These discussions have the appearance of strengthening, but actually result in shrinking us and making us weaker.

But the learning that helps us to do better next time is liberating and growth producing. The courage to conduct an autopsy leads to healthier and more cohesive teams, better results next time, and increased confidence in individual leaders. Honesty has a way of making things stronger over time.

And that's got hope written all over it.

the problem with *T-shirts*

RECENTLY I READ SOME statistics on the Internet that said in order to stay aligned with a company's vision, people need to be reminded of that vision every twenty-eight days. I'm not sure how they came up with twenty-eight days; seems like a strange number to me. But suffice it to say, people need to hear about the vision on a regular basis in order to stay motivated.

Great leaders think about vision—a lot. But the problem is that most of us are thinking about it more than we are talking about it. And if vision is that important, we need to be constantly asking ourselves, *What's our vision, and how are we doing at communicating it?*

In many organizations, once a vision statement is crafted, it's often written on a piece of paper and put in a notebook, only brought out again a couple of times a year at new employee orientation or in a leader's speech. Occasionally it might make its way onto a mug or a T-shirt.

Nothing inspires cynicism in an organization faster than a T-shirt.

Vision doesn't belong on T-shirts. As leaders, our job is to breathe life into the vision and fill the words with meaning that stirs people in the deepest parts of their souls—the parts that long for meaning, significance, and transformation. We need to come up with creative, compelling, and repetitive ways to talk about the vision, and then we need to make the words come alive. Sometimes we even need to say those words in different ways so that people can see every facet of the vision, like the shifting colors of a kaleidoscope.

Vision is about stirring and provoking, reminding and imagining. It's about showing people the wonder of an improved future and infusing them with hope. Vision is about creating a reason to believe again.

Vision is primarily nurtured through the stories we tell and the heroes we create in our organizations. A couple of years ago, our consulting team was working with a large school district on the East Coast. We were in the second day of a two-day off-site conference, with about a hundred and twenty people around tables in a large room. As is true with any school district, this one was facing huge challenges: increasing ethnic and economic diversity in its student population, budget cuts, and mounting expectations in test scores.

As part of an exercise in vision, we asked people to stand up and tell a brief story or mention a hero who reflected the district's vision of "providing a place where every child can succeed."

The principal for one of the larger high schools in the district stood up and talked about a young African American boy who

Vision is primarily nurtured through the stories we tell and the heroes we create in our organizations.

had just graduated the month before. He had spent six years, from middle school through high school, in the district, but he stood out from the other kids because he was homeless—by choice.

Although this boy had received numerous offers of housing from friends, he did not want to be separated from his mother, so for nearly six years he woke up every morning in the backseat of a car. He walked across the parking lot to a nearby Wal-Mart, where he washed up in the restrooms. Then he took two city buses to arrive at school before the first bell rang. He ended up graduating with a Bill and Melinda Gates Foundation scholarship, a full ride to a four-year college of his choice.

The story took two minutes to tell. But by the end, I was ready to quit my job and go to work for that school district.

Here's the deal. No one goes into education for the big paycheck. That two-minute story worked in a powerful way to reconnect those overworked and underpaid educators to the core reason that had brought them into this line of work in the first place. You could see it all over the room: tender smiles, nodding heads, people clearly reenergized and ready to return to the issues of diversity, budget, and test scores with a renewed sense of purpose and hope. The story was a creative and compelling way to remind people of the vision.

Two minutes.

Some of my most memorable intersections with powerful vision have come in educational contexts. Perhaps it's because there is no question that something more than money motivates educators. Another time, we were working with a large school district in the Los Angeles area. Once again we were focusing on the topic of vision, but this time, we had divided the group into teams: administrators, principals, psychologists, teachers, etc. One team in particular worried me: the facilities and maintenance employees. I wasn't at all sure that these guys in their jeans and T-shirts would be able to deeply engage in a discussion about vision. After all, their primary responsibilities included cutting the grass and cleaning the bathrooms.

Vision is about stirring and provoking, reminding and imagining.

I can be an idiot sometimes, but that's for another chapter.

After I explained what I wanted the teams to do, I walked over to "help" this table. I kneeled down and said in my best consulting voice, "So, what have you got for me?"

The head of the department said, "Well, I've been thinking about this idea a lot over the past twenty-five years," and the rest of the guys around the table chuckled. I assumed he was having a hard time figuring out this vision thing, so I continued, "Well, tell me what you have been thinking."

To this day, I still carry a scrap of paper in my wallet on which I've written what that man said next:

"We work to create and maintain an environment that inspires greatness."

"Excuse me?"

As he repeated that sentence (that glorious sentence)

the laughter around the table returned, and stories started spilling out.

"Yeah, yeah, we don't just plant flowers, we create gardens that inspire greatness," one of them said playfully.

As if trying to top that, another said, "When people use the bathroom, they will look around the facility with a pride that comes from cleanliness and working parts all in order."

"Everywhere people look, everything they see, from the grass to the classrooms to the restrooms, will inspire them toward greatness because of the physical environment of the schools. From the teachers to the students to the parents, even the FedEx guys that make deliveries on our campuses . . ." I was getting the picture.

Wow. After I steadied myself from having been bowled over, I stood up from my kneeling position. Then I bowed down to them.

I returned to the front of the room and told the entire group what had just happened. I said, "These guys are rock stars! If the facilities and maintenance guys can come to work every day understanding that their job is about more than trimming shrubs and cleaning toilets, that it's up to them to create an environment that inspires greatness, then everyone in this organization should be able to figure out how to tie his or her job to the vision.

"You all ought to bow down every time you cross paths with one of these men. We are not worthy to look directly into their eyes; we ought to give them sunglasses so we can pass by," I finished with a smile.

The next time we worked with this district, the superintendent told us we had created monsters! The maintenance guys now strutted through the campuses . . . and well they should.

Heroes like this shape the culture of an organization, giving its vision form and substance and breathing life into it. They turn an organization into a living entity, taking it out of the "institution" category and plopping it squarely into the "organism" category.

It is good for us to think about organizations as living things, because doing so moves us away from the idea that it's us—people—against the organization. We need to realize that the organization *is* the people.

The right heroes help us fight the encroaching celebrity culture that can destroy even the best organizations: that not-so-subtle elevation of jocks and cheerleaders that leaves everyone else feeling like second-class citizens, minor contributors, or page-3 news.

We need heroes to give flesh and bone to the vision, helping people see what's right in front of their eyes. And the best heroes make everyone else in the organization realize that "hero-hood" is not reserved for the select few, but that they, too, can become heroes. And maybe, just maybe, vision is a collection of heroes that point us all in the right direction.

I have attended a lot of meetings where sales and marketing people are given awards. They get the verbal accolades and the nodding approvals; all the while the data entry person who made the success possible—or at least had a lot to do with it—sits unnoticed in the corner. Good leaders make sure no one is overlooked. That might sound like it's too big a job. Well, it *is* a big job, but it's not too big. It is imperative, and one of the primary ways of realizing vision. And it is the right thing to do, which is so much of what leadership is about.

Much of a vision's power lies in what it taps into. Done well, vision connects to that part of us that desperately wants to be involved in something deeper, something with meaning and significance. Vision releases ongoing energy in individuals and organizations that perpetuates and fuels itself. Vision lifts heads, stirs souls, and taps hearts. It creates and fosters and strengthens and stimulates. It engages passion, which is a profound source of motivation. Vision brings out the best, where before, good enough was good enough.

Right now, our firm is working with an agency in a

nearby community that's been ravaged by violence and is struggling to overcome the legacy of destruction left behind. For years, this area had the highest murder rate per capita in the state, and for a while, in the country. It is difficult and sometimes discouraging work. Two steps forward, five steps back. Recently the community experienced shootings for thirty days in a row. Thirty days, every day a shooting—some fatal, some not.

They are working to create avenues of nonviolence in this community. They've started programs in the schools and the neighborhoods to target susceptible kids and intervene in this seemingly endless cycle. The agency does good work. The people there teach classes, they counsel, they offer music and art lessons, they host a weekly family night, and they try to "reprogram" the community mind-set that sees violence as a way of life.

The young staff that so passionately leads this organization tries to be relationally available to the people of the community 24-7. What they do is so important, and in this area, they are the only ones doing it. They frequently gather as a group to remind themselves of their vision. They tell stories of the successes and celebrate every step in the right direction. When discouragement seeps in, as it does on a regular basis, they return to their vision. They remind themselves of the truth and hope of the words. Their heroes are those who are living out the vision. When they get weary of doing good, it is not the strategy or logistics or budget that breathes life back into their understandably worn-out souls. It is the vision. It is the stories.

Not the vision on a T-shirt, but the vision as it is lived out in the flesh and blood of those within their God-blessed reach.

stone *Ships*

HAVE YOU EVER HEARD the phrase "There is no such thing as a bad idea"?

Maybe there is.

Here's what leaders know about bad ideas: From time to time, they happen; and the fear of them can keep organizations from doing the risk taking and creative thinking necessary to keep those organizations innovative and growing. When the fear of a bad idea is big enough, it paralyzes people.

We talk a lot of the need to take risks, to think outside the box, to try new things. We know we need to keep organizations fresh and growing and that can't be accomplished by only doing the same old things.

But while we talk a good game, most of us also feel the undercurrent in those words: "Feel free to succeed."

Stone ships.

In many organizations, mistakes are met with awkward silences, punishing behavior, and a distinct sense of being marginalized and labeled. The embarrassment becomes a legacy rather than an event.

On the other hand, "successes" are applauded and extolled, heroes are created and parties are thrown. We learn pretty quickly which side we need to be on.

Now, before I go on, let me make clear what I'm not saying. It's obviously not a good idea to fail on purpose, to let bad ideas go unchecked, or to abdicate discernment in exchange for creativity. What I *am* saying is this: We need to create environments in our organizations where creativity and new ideas can flourish.

We all want to avoid stone ships, but our fear of them keeps us doing the same things in the same way, year after year. And everyone who leads well will have a few stone ships in his or her past, and maybe one or two in the future.

Leading an organization requires a collaborative discussion about vision, reality, and strategy. And while I am not one for linear leadership, this is one discussion that needs to at least begin in that order.

The leader starts by orchestrating a team dialogue about what the future might look like: How might our organization flourish in the future? Where are we going? What are the ways in which new life must be breathed into what we are doing?

Beyond the central leadership team, these discussions then need to move out into the organization. People from various areas and departments need to participate in the conversation about what the future might look like and where they want the organization to go. These discussions, in and of themselves, have the potential to release the energy inside people. The dreaming creates it, and the invitation to the conversation releases it. Good leaders know that an entire culture can be ignited by the discussion about what's next.

Leading an organization requires a collaborative discussion about vision, reality, and strategy.

Many leaders are afraid of opening up this type of dialogue. But sometimes fearing the wrong things can actually hurt us. And *not* having these widespread discussions ought to make us afraid.

Collaboration is not abdication. Collaboration releases the energy and passions and unique contributions of people made in the image of God. It is a dynamic force that most leaders often vastly undervalue and therefore underutilize.

Collaboration is not a promise; it is an invitation. Hearing people does not mandate that you will always follow what they say. But it is a significant way for you to value and engage people. It brings issues to the surface that need to be tackled (which is one reason most people prefer to avoid it), but more importantly it creates a shared vision that ignites the imagination and efforts of the entire team.

Vision is a team sport. It is not a solo endeavor. Far too often, leaders present their vision to a group and then get confused when the progress seems slow or people are reluctant. Very few people are motivated when they are handed a vision. Most want to be part of determining and shaping that vision. And when you invite people to the table with you to do that, you deeply honor their dignity and the image of God embedded within them.

Good leaders create momentum not just in the execution of the vision, but in the dis-

Vision is a team sport.

cussions leading up to the vision. I see a lot of leaders who spend enormous amounts of energy trying to rally the troops and get people fired up to implement the leaders' vision. Even from simply a practical point of view, they would save themselves a boatload of effort if they engaged people from the beginning rather than after the vision was decided.

This process of determining vision can seem like it

takes too long, but I would submit that exactly the opposite is true. Pushing people is a lot more work than running along with them. When you ask them the questions and involve them in shaping the future, you treat them like partners, not subjects.

We spent nearly a year shaping our vision at Axis (to state the obvious, we did not set aside our regular ministry work while we were doing this). We involved not just our leadership team, but scores of key volunteers and regular attendees in the discussions. We began by gathering groups of people and asking three questions:

1. What is going so well in the ministry that you'd like us not to touch it for fear we might mess it up?
2. What is broken and either needs fixing or needs to be shut down?
3. What are the things we are not yet doing that we ought to consider for our future?

People were honored to be invited, excited to be asked, and full of ideas to the point of bursting. Those three questions and the opportunity to talk about them together catalyzed an energy within the group that was palpable. We probed their answers, took notes, and paid off our promise to keep them updated.

We took our staff and interns away for a couple of retreats where we considered the information we had gathered at these group events. We prayed, we talked, we listened. And after considerable time, we wrote:

> Axis strives to be a vibrant, authentic community of Jesus followers who seek to impact our world by helping our friends discover Jesus and serving our neighbors in need.
>
> Community. Evangelism. Serving.

I remember being in the living room of a friend's house overlooking Lake Michigan when about twenty of us looked at that statement on a flip chart. There was a brief silence as we saw it and took it in, then an excitement began to fill the room with an immediate sense of "Let's get started!"

We weren't looking at months of "rolling it out" to people who would be hearing it for the first time, but rather we were trying to steer the energy and direction of people who had been an integral part of creating it and who were already chomping at the bit to get started.

Personally, I would rather lead people I have to pull back and steer a bit than those who need a constant fire lit under them. Welcoming collaboration from the start is a significant way to create the former situation.

But vision is just the first part. Next comes reality. Reality isn't nearly as much fun as vision, but it is quite necessary. In fact, my mentor Max DePree says that the first job of a leader is to define reality. Max and I may disagree just a bit on the order, but suffice it to say that vision doesn't happen without considering your current reality.

It takes a lot of courage from a leader to accurately assess current reality. One of the reasons that is true is that to a large degree, the leader is responsible for the current reality. Only new leaders can avoid that responsibility, and sooner or later we all have to get comfortable with owning our failures as well as our successes.

Assessing the current reality almost always involves bad news. It includes hearing about what is not working, what or who has lost effectiveness, and ways in which people have felt marginalized, used, and overlooked. Current reality includes details about systems or programs that no longer deliver what they were originally intended to, as well as places where the organization is stuck.

This is one of the reasons why leadership is so much work. The vision is full of possibilities and optimism. Reality is more often filled with disappointments and difficulties. And a leader needs to stand between those two things.

It is so much easier to choose one or the other. Tension

implies pulling—and when does that feel good? The tendency to move to the either/or is often driven by the desire to avoid that pain. But leadership doesn't allow for that luxury. It requires the orchestration of opposites. The space between the vision and reality creates a gap, a painful gap. And leadership is about bridging that gap. More on that later . . .

In Axis, we soberly and honestly assessed our current reality. But before we did, we coached ourselves on the importance of engaging in this part of the discussion with a ruthless honesty. If we held back, we knew we would not come to the correct conclusions. If protecting feelings was our highest value, we would miss the truth. Fortunately, our enthusiasm for moving toward the vision helped us garner the necessary courage to do what needed to be done.

Our discoveries were painful, but interestingly, they were also remarkably freeing. In the face of our vision, the very things that initially seemed scary and hard to admit became great tools for overcoming the obstacles that were blocking our future.

Our weekend service was one of the most important things we did each week. We began to see how these services had become predictable more than provocative. Now that we understood our vision, we realized that the services weren't as focused or participatory as they needed to be.

Our small groups were mostly superficial and were not being led very well. Many of them were stagnant, and few were growing. We knew we needed to make the ties between our weekend services and our small groups much stronger and clearer.

Then we looked at serving. Okay, well, our current reality was that there was no current reality in the area of serving. There were some random acts of serving, but not much beyond that. Serving was not a force in our community.

Rather than being collaborative and interconnected, the areas within Axis were more like silos. The various teams that worked during the weekend services constantly struggled to find enough help, and few people in Axis were actively building friendships with people who didn't know God.

The intersection of vision and reality may be one of the greatest tests of leadership.

Did I mention that reality hurts? Who wants to hear all that stuff? This intersection of vision and reality may be one of the greatest tests of leadership. It is having sober eyes and an optimistic spirit, and refusing to choose between the two. It is the good news–bad news moment when you cannot allow one to dismiss the other. They are both true—where we are heading and where we are—but we have to walk through reality in order to move toward the vision. Without that, vision becomes a simple addiction to the emotional high of an imagined future.

Vision is hard work. Stinking hard work. And living in reality prepares us for that. It takes us out of the clouds and puts us in work boots. We dream and we struggle. We seek to bring the Kingdom of God into a world that is not yet ready for all of it. The tension between these two things is the realm of good leadership. Discouragement and belief: strange but necessary bedfellows.

One of the most painful things about a disappointing reality is that at one time, those things that are now not working originated under the banner of a glorious vision. There must be a continual monitoring of the vision against the current reality.

The disparity between the vision and the reality establishes a gap. And what fills that gap is strategy. Strategy answers the "how" question: How will we move from our current reality to our preferred future? Without a plan, the gap will remain.

Of course there will always be a gap, but strategy is about pointing the way and narrowing the gap. Strategy focuses on the two, three, maybe four main things that we have determined will significantly move us toward our vision. It builds a bridge between here and there, between the real and the anticipated. And bridges are full of hope.

Strategy puts feet to the vision and, as such, breathes encouragement into an organization as it takes its first steps toward the future. Strategy gives us the potential to move our organizations from having a soft, benign presence in the community to being unstoppable forces in our world. It brings a focus and clarity to our flurry of activities and our wonderful random acts of kindness—and that unleashes power.

Strategy puts feet to the vision and, as such, breathes encouragement into an organization as it takes its first steps toward the future.

Because there are thousands of wonderful causes, we must do the work of determining what we will spend our great but limited resources of time, energy, and money on. We must ask, is the cause effective and sustainable? In doing this, we create the possibility of releasing those resources in remarkable and not-to-be-ignored ways. I think part of what Jesus meant when He told Peter that the gates of hell would not prevail against His church is the kind of strength that can be created when God's people come together focused on both the dream and the reality.

It is tempting to say yes to everything—particularly for those working in churches and nonprofit organizations. I once did some work with the leadership team of a small church with about a hundred and fifty in its congregation. We did a strategy exercise in which I asked the team to list the various ministries within the church. I finally stopped writing when we had filled up an entire whiteboard. This small church had seventy-five different activities going! That's a ministry for every two people in the church. Easy to see strategic mistakes in someone else, isn't it?

In Axis, our strategy very simply became large group gatherings, small-group gatherings, and serving opportunities. Just those three things. Other great ideas came our way all the time, but our strategy gave us the confidence to say no, thank you.

We decided that we would become a vibrant community of Jesus followers, we would become active in helping our friends discover Jesus, and we would serve our neighbors in need through these three strategic anchors. Everything that happened, then, in our large and small-group gatherings and through our serving opportunities needed to direct people to growth in those three areas.

So we knew that our weekend services needed to be transformational and point people both to our great God and to His community. They needed to be creative, relevant, and provocative in order to engage and move people. We began to highlight serving opportunities and the stories that emerged from them in our services.

Our small-group leaders needed to be trained in an ongoing manner. That training needed to be authentic and done in community. Our leaders needed to be envisioned and trained to lead groups where people could be known and transformed. Jesus needed to be at the center of these times, and serving opportunities needed to become a part of the rhythm of each home group as well.

Regular serving opportunities, both through home groups and Axis-wide events, needed to become a regular part of the fabric of Axis.

Transformational large group events.

Transformational small-group gatherings.

Transformational serving opportunities.

Three areas of focus, consistently given our best efforts, prayers, and ideas.

Building into the people who would lead each of those areas.

When you build an organization through a collaborative vision that honestly assesses current reality, you'll find that the number of stone ships you encounter decreases. Somewhere along the way, someone will have the courage to tell you that while a ship is a great idea, you might want to reconsider the building material.

But remember this: Avoiding stone ships is not the goal. The goal is creating an organization that flourishes and thrives, that creates and transforms, and that becomes a force to change things and help people.

Seabiscuit

FOR A LOT OF REASONS, I was not the most obvious or anticipated choice when it came to leading Axis, a ministry that
was geared to the "eighteen to twentysomething generation." For starters, I was a middle-aged woman, and to my
knowledge, that was not at the top of the list of qualifica-
tions the Axis team wanted in its next leader. Axis had
been started, appropriately so, by a guy who was edgy and
postmodern.

Edgy and postmodern and young.

They got me.

I'm sure they weren't thrilled when I came on board, and
least thrilled of all was Steve. As the program director, Steve

oversaw the teams that put the weekend service together. That service formed the bedrock of our ministry and was among the most important things we produced week after week. Steve had been doing this job almost since Axis began.

He was distant and suspicious of me—polite, but barely. He avoided and questioned me, which is a lovely combination (the tone you're sensing there is my spiritual gift of sarcasm, finely honed over time). My first week on the job, I asked him, "When does the programming team meet?"

A simple, innocuous question. I was the leader of Axis, Axis held a weekend service, and the programming team designed, planned, and executed that service. I should probably know when the meeting was so that I wouldn't be late.

"We don't need you at that meeting," Steve replied. Since then, Steve and I have had many a good laugh over that, but I wasn't laughing that day.

I didn't realize it at the time, but some of his reticence toward me was a reaction to leaders in the past who had come to that meeting, taken over, and changed everything. And I don't think that was all that was going on. Steve wasn't thrilled about me as the new leader of Axis, quite possibly because he was hoping he might get the job, but certainly because he never expected they would give it to someone his parents' age.

While my response to Steve was that I would be coming to each and every one of the programming meetings, I also did something else. Although I was pretty miffed, I tried to imagine what it would be like to be in Steve's shoes. Here he was, in his midtwenties and absolutely passionate about designing a church experience that would reach his friends—friends who either hadn't given church a second thought since third grade or had never given church a thought at all. Steve had a whole generation of friends who didn't know what Jesus said, even though they thought He was a swell guy.

And for a couple of years before my arrival, Axis had been doing a good job at carving out a place for those people. Then they got me as their new leader. I think I understood the problem.

Slowly, over the next year, we built trust. It was rarely easy, and it took a lot of difficult conversations, the kind that don't often occur in church settings. But I think Steve began to see that I was just as passionate about his generation as he was. He saw that I was more collaborative than hierarchical, and that I believed deeply in leadership development as a key and necessary component of leadership.

He saw that I could support and get excited about

someone else's ideas and that I could make mistakes and wasn't afraid to own them.

It was difficult on my end as well as I tried to walk the awkward line of understanding a generation that I wasn't a member of. I told my staff early on that if I ever came to work wearing leather pants they could fire me on the spot. They didn't even have to check with the elders.

During one of my first programming meetings, I found myself listening as the team got excited about doing a Barenaked Ladies song that weekend in the service. Keeping an absolutely straight face, with a slight approving nod so as not to appear completely uncool, I left the meeting and quickly called one of my daughters.

"Yeah, Mom, totally okay. Sounds bad, but actually a really great choice."

Thanks, Mallory.

So we did this funky dance for at least six months. Two different generations, who leads?

There is a great scene in the movie *Seabiscuit* that applies to this idea. The main character, Red Pollard, is the jockey who has been riding Seabiscuit to victory. He knows the horse so well that his riding is intuitive. But Red is involved in a disastrous accident that leaves him incapacitated for months.

From his hospital bed, he coaches the new jockey about

how to ride his horse. And he lets him in on a little secret, a secret that comes from knowing the animal in a way no one else does.

"Keep him back a little. Let him feel the race, the track, and the other horses. And then, at the right time, get him neck and neck with another horse, one that has fire, and let him look directly into his eyes. When he locks eyes with that horse, Seabiscuit will take off."

For months during his recovery, Red listens and watches as this other jockey rides his horse, until the day finally comes that he is deemed fit to ride again. Although he is in excruciating pain, Red pulls his broken and wounded body up onto his beloved horse.

To his surprise, as he rides toward the starting gate, he sees the other jockey riding up on another horse. They greet each other and move into position. The excitement and chaos of those prerace moments fills the air. And then the bell sounds, the gate goes up, and the thunderous roar of the horses begins.

Almost immediately, Red is feeling the groan and ache of his shattered body, bones knit back together but still rebelling as they bear the weight of the jockey and control the horse. It becomes clear that Red is not able to ride in a way that will propel Seabiscuit to victory.

And then, there he is. The other jockey. He sees what

is happening and he pulls his horse back. On purpose. He pulls his horse back and waits until Seabiscuit gets neck and neck, eye level with him. He waits for just a moment, for Seabiscuit to get what he needs. Then he says to Red, "Enjoy the race; see you at the finish line."

And Seabiscuit pulls ahead, first over the line.

It was a great moment in the movie, but more than that, I think it is a picture of great leadership. Those of us who have gone ahead and have been doing this for a while need to pull back. On purpose. We need to position ourselves beside those who are coming up and may be struggling a bit. We need to give what we can of ourselves to let others move ahead.

Those of us who have gone ahead and have been doing this for a while need to pull back. On purpose.

Those of us who have been building organizations or ministries or teams need to stop and put others on our shoulders in order to provide them with a better view than even we have. And then we say to them—in hushed tones—"Tell me what you see."

It is always a tension, leading for now and for the future, slowing down enough to develop and bring along new, young leaders. But it may be one of the most important things we do as leaders as we identify, teach and train, bless and release the next generation(s) of leaders.

We have to trust that in their own way they have much to offer, things that we cannot bring to the table. So while we lead them, we must also honor them and believe in them, cheering them on as we pull ourselves back and watch them race ahead.

In addition to a great staff of eleven employees, Axis also had about seven or eight interns who were part of a larger intern program at Willow Creek. When they were in our area, I was responsible for these additional people who gave greatly of their time and energy and giftedness to help grow and develop our ministry.

I was a great fan of the internship program. Although these young people were only required to spend twenty hours in our department, each and every one of them gave much more than was required. They were motivated, sincere, passionate leaders, excited beyond belief to be a part of Axis.

With no budget requirement on my part, I had extra leadership help in spades; what was not to like? Well, sometimes the interns made me tired. They were young and had a lot to learn. They made mistakes and messes, and they needed direction and guidance and discipleship and training. I realized that to give them what they needed, I would have to slow down a bit, pull beside them. Sometimes that was okay with me, but mostly I found myself getting annoyed. To be painfully honest, I would have rather been given the extra leadership horsepower without having to do any additional work on my part.

I know, I know, you've never felt that way.

One day, I sat down with my boss and told him what I was feeling. I explained that although I was a huge fan of the internship program, some days I was just irritated by the burden of it and the way it slowed us down. I really had a good complaint session, confession being good for the soul and all. And my boss, he just listened. Listened and nodded. Surprisingly, I felt a bit better just having said what was on my mind.

One of the things I love about the Holy Spirit is that sometimes His conviction is just a gentle grain of sand that settles into our hearts where it scratches and irritates until we finally do something about it. And when I left my boss's office that day, the Holy Spirit went with me.

Of course I know He always goes with me, but that day He just gently hung around until my own words echoed in my head and choked in my throat. With slow realization, the selfishness of my attitude became fully clear, and I was ashamed. Not the kind of shame that occurs because everyone knows you've done something wrong. Until I wrote this chapter, no one except my boss and me ever knew about that conversation.

No, this was the kind of shame that emerges strong and hard, even though you know that no one else may ever know.

My boss never brought up the subject, but a few months later, I did. After referring back to that conversation, I told him I no longer felt that way. He smiled slightly and asked why.

I told him I had heard a whisper that day. Sometimes the Spirit of God is a loud wind, but other days He is just a still, small voice. And that voice reminded me that when I was nineteen years old and volunteering in the high school group at my church, a youth pastor named Jamie Barr let me make mistakes and messes, and he discipled me when I needed direction and guidance and training. He slowed down, pulled beside me, taught me, listened to me, and let me take off.

That was the only reminder I needed. I was reminded of Jamie Barr and I was grateful. And gratitude freed me to do the same for someone else.

One of the best gifts you can give to new leaders as you develop them is the freedom to learn from you, and then to do things their own way. Much damage has been done to new leaders when older, more seasoned ones insist on clones. I have seen too many young leaders who look disturbingly like mini-me versions of their mentors. There is a delicate dance between imparting the wisdom you have gained from experience and trying to mold someone else into your own likeness.

The writer of 1 Samuel captures this tension beautifully in chapter 17. The army of Israel is stationed on the edge of a ravine, holding ground but not advancing against the Philistines. On the other side is Goliath, spokesman-elect by virtue of his size and strength. In a loud, taunting voice, Goliath mocks the Israelites for their cowardice and invites someone—anyone—to come forward and fight him, proving which is the stronger army and nation, and therefore who follows the bigger and better God.

Israel's army is nearly paralyzed by Goliath's presence, and David, who has been sent to deliver news and food to his brothers, is simply mortified that no one is doing anything. He can't believe they are allowing this bully to verbally abuse their God, and insists that he be allowed to stand up against the giant.

It seems, from reading this passage, that there is a tremendous undercurrent here. Sure, King Saul is probably a bit embarrassed by David's suggestion of action in the face of his own passive attitude, but he also finds him amusing, perhaps even scrappy. David is a nice diversion, someone to take everyone's minds off the fear-inducing Goliath.

But after laughing at him, Saul sees that David is not

to be dissuaded, so he humors him. *Okay, sure, little guy, I admire your spunk. Here, if you insist on going after the giant, at least let me lend you my protective gear. I have a helmet and a sword, chest armor and a shield. They're a little big, but that's because they belong to me, and I am big and you are not. But you will need them, so here, let me help you get that on over your head.*

Perhaps those who are watching snicker at the ludicrous sight of David clomping and tromping and stumbling and tripping in the heavy metal protection. But David is more focused on conserving his energy to defend the God of Israel. In 1 Samuel 17:39, we see him stop and say, with great clarity and courage: "I cannot go in these . . . because I am not used to them."

From a strategic point of view, that might possibly be one of the stupidest responses in the Bible. Inexperienced and ill-equipped, David chooses to remove the protective armor. The armor worked for Saul, but it would only be a burden for David, hampering his movements. David decides to stick with what he knows. He grabs his shepherd's staff and sling, and picks up five smooth stones from the river, stones just like the ones he had used to kill bears and lions that had threatened his sheep. David chooses to fight Goliath as the shepherd God has made him to be, not as the soldier-king that Saul is.

The rest of the story speaks for itself, but it is easy to miss the courage it took for David to say, "I cannot go in these because I am not used to them."

I guess the question for those of us who do leadership development is this: Do we have the courage to make room for people to do it their way? By insisting on that, we honor the individual that God made each person to be. We free ourselves from making people over in our image for our own validation.

To be sure, an enormous part of developing leaders is about teaching and training. We cannot do it without imparting truths out of our own learning and wisdom. Here we are again, at that increasingly familiar place of tension. But in addition to imparting our wisdom, we can encourage people to do things their way. We can ask the question "What do you think?" We can allow for mistakes and room for different ways of approaching issues.

As leaders, we need to offer the armor, but smile when others try it on and politely decline. We watch in amazement as those we lead approach a problem differently than we might, but solve it well. We get excited when the direction and freedom we provide leads to fresh, new change. And we grow ourselves when we realize that this learning process is beautifully reciprocal.

A number of years ago, a young man named David

Hubbard became the president of Fuller Seminary. He was the youngest man to have ever taken that post. One of the gifts God gave David to help him lead well was Max DePree. Max was a successful business leader who came alongside David and offered him six words.

Six powerful words.

"I am committed to your success."

And then Max, a Fortune 500 company president, moved joyfully into the shadows. He positioned himself behind David.

From behind the scenes we can say, "If you need me, I'm right here. From time to time, I will whisper in your ear some of the most significant things

"I am committed to your success."

that God has been good enough to teach me. You can decide what you need. From time to time I will stand next to you and I will speak encouragement and a call to persevere, because sometimes that is just what a leader needs.

"I will believe in the gifts and ability and character that I see in you, and I will point you to the God who is the giver of all of those things. I am steadfastly devoted and faithfully committed to you as the leader of this place."

When someone who is a little further down the road than you are stands behind and beside you like that, it spurs you on. It's exciting at my age to see young leaders learning, apprenticing, and then striking out on their own. And it's even more exciting to look around at the rest of us who are giving, teaching, directing, and celebrating as we all head toward the same finish line.

Together.

Rock, Paper, Scissors

PERHAPS ONE OF THE most powerful things a leader can do is to deeply value the contributions of everyone in the organization. Unfortunately, many leaders have bought into the celebrity culture (I don't have time to cover it here, but when a nineteen-year-old pop star makes more in one appearance than the average schoolteacher can hope to make in a lifetime, we need a new culture). When contributions are unfairly measured against each other, it creates an environment of favorites and pits those who ought to be collaborative colleagues against one another in destructive ways.

It is not reasonable to assume that janitors will be

financially compensated along the lines of the CEO, but an equal valuing of contributions is not about money. In fact, it doesn't have to cost anything at all. And the power it creates in an organization can be amazing.

For a number of years, I worked as a nurse in a large hospital in the Orange County area of Southern California. For part of that time I was assigned to the emergency department. Every day was different, and most of the time, the work was interesting and action packed. But some days were definitely better than others, and it all depended on which of the doctors was working that shift.

I was not alone in my assessment. Any time we came to work and found this particular doctor on duty, we all knew it was going to be a great shift. Why? Because that man knew how to value people. He knew how to bring a disparate group of coworkers together and orchestrate us to function like a great team. He knew how to appreciate the unique contribution that each member made, and he knew how to call it out of us. Those eight-hour shifts flew by when he was in charge.

This was no small challenge in our department because often in an emergency situation, the team involved wasn't a group of people who regularly functioned together. A few of us from the ER formed the core of the team, but we were often joined by someone from the lab, radiology, respiratory therapy, or translator teams, to name a few.

One evening we had spent nearly four hours working on a patient. It was unclear until about the last half hour whether we would be sending her upstairs to intensive care or downstairs to the morgue. Her condition was touch and go for a long time, and we were both exhilarated and exhausted by the time we wheeled her and her myriad of tubes upstairs.

During the code situation, this doctor had done what he did best. He asked for input from the various people on the team. He never gave us the sense that because he was the doctor, he felt entitled to decide everything for himself. When doing so did not in any way endanger the speed of care, he asked what we thought was going on or what to do next. And yet, even though he asked these types of questions, he never abdicated his role as team leader.

He complimented team members on a good IV start or a clear X-ray that aided in a quick and accurate diagnosis. He thanked people for their contribution during the action, and used the words *great job* over and over throughout the situation. In addition, he was quick to coach and correct when needed. We all welcomed that because with him as our leader, we *wanted* to grow and do better.

After the gurney was in the elevator, I went back to the

room we had been working in. Just a few minutes earlier, the room had looked like a hurricane had gone through it, but now it was already clean and ready for the next patient. I was alone in the room, finishing up some documentation, when the doctor came back in. He was accompanied by an intern who had been his sidekick during the code. Oblivious to my presence, the doctor walked this young doctor-to-be through the experience, both encouraging him for the things he had done correctly and offering direction and alternatives for areas he felt had been lacking.

I was doing what any good nurse would do in a similar situation: eavesdropping. Then the doctor said something to the intern that I will never forget: "When the code was over, did you notice the young man from housekeeping who came in and cleaned up this whirlwind mess?"

You could tell by the look on the intern's face that not only had he *not* noticed, but he also had no idea why he was being asked this seemingly irrelevant question. I guess irrelevance is in the eye of the beholder.

The doctor went on. "His name is Carlos. And he is one of the best workers in the entire housekeeping department. When Carlos comes in during or after a code, he gets the room cleaned up so quickly that we can immediately take another patient in the space."

The blank expression on the intern's face told the doctor

that he still had little to no level of understanding of the point of all this. So the doctor continued. "Carlos came up from Mexico about three years ago. His wife's name is Maria, and they have four kids." He then went on to name the children as well as their ages.

"They live in a small rented house in Santa Ana, about three miles from here. The next time we work together, I would like you to tell me something about Carlos that I don't already know. Okay, let's go, we've got other patients waiting."

Sometimes you get to watch breathtaking leadership.

When we play favorites, everyone knows what's going on. It is demotivating at best, and devaluing at worst. Most likely you know exactly what I mean, because most of us have worked for leaders who play favorites. It's so obvious it is palpable, yet no one admits it. And this makes the game all the more crazy-making.

Great leaders know the value of doing the right thing, and that includes valuing the contribution of all the players. The power that is released in a culture that values collaboration is so great to see. A leader who knows names, knows individual stories, and honors the role of each person reflexively brings out the best contribution possible.

Obviously the caveat here is that any one given leader can only know so many people. But even in large organizations

I have seen leaders do a great job with this. There are many different ways to do it; what matters is that you do it.

One leader I know in the business field asks his direct reports to tell him about a manager or administrative or janitorial staff member who has done a great job recently. He asks them to give him as many specifics as they can. And then he sets aside fifteen minutes every week to leave a voice mail, detailing the behavior and thanking those people for the ways in which they did their jobs in those instances.

He leaves it on their voice mail at home.

I love that. They would certainly expect it more on their work voice mail, but imagine coming home after a long day, hitting the play button, and hearing the president of the institution you work for congratulating you for something you did that week. And then thanking you for helping to create a great organization.

That's just one way of valuing collaboration. There are a lot of ways to notice people, especially people whose jobs do not put them in the limelight often, whose work often goes unnoticed and unappreciated. People get weary doing that kind of job week in and week out. They begin to feel as if they are in the middle of a giant game of rock, paper, scissors. Just when they think they are the rock, along comes paper . . . and they lose.

Great leaders refuse to play that game. They find ways

to notice, to appreciate, to praise, to thank. They don't do it in ways that manipulate or control. They authentically understand that everyone has a job to do, and when someone does it well, it should not be overlooked. Max DePree often reminds board members that they should know at least one name of someone who works on the cleaning staff—his or her name and story. Powerful stuff, not to be underestimated.

Funny how doing the right thing so often goes hand in hand with releasing astonishing power in both people and organizations.

It is easy to forget this and to start weighing the contributions of people according to what *you* value, or even based on what *you* would have done in their situations. "Be like me and you will get attention" is often a forceful but unspoken value in a corporate culture or ministry environment. Great leaders push themselves to understand the unique and valuable contributions of everyone on the team.

I remember vividly an Axis meeting where we were faced with a problem. It was a significant issue, and the meeting included a mix of staff and key volunteer leaders. As I explained the problem and my desire to use this meeting to talk about problem solving, I noticed that the guy sitting across from me had that "whenever you stop talking, I have something to say" look. Surprised that he didn't find my vision casting so compelling that he completely forgot what he was going to say, I called on him when I finished.

Right away he said, "I've been thinking, and I have a plan sort of sketched out. Would you mind if I drew it up on the whiteboard and quickly talked us through it?"

Mind? Well, yes. First you need to acknowledge that what I have just said is the most brilliant contribution to this problem to date. It was like he hadn't even heard a word I had been saying. It was like his mind, and his own unique perspective, had been launched into work even as I was still talking.

And the worst of it was this: His idea was terrific. No, seriously. I mean his layout of a strategic plan, divided into timelines, with specific names by each area, was amazing both in its scope and its potential to solve this problem. Actually, maybe the worst of it was that I wasn't the only person to notice it. Everyone else around the room was vigorously nodding their approval and admiration.

I should have been ecstatic. I knew that. I should have been delighted that in such a short time, such a great mind had done the work of wrapping itself around the dilemma and coming up with a workable solution. Except that I was jealous. (At this point, I am thinking about publishing this book under an assumed name.) How pathetic was my response?

While the green-eyed monster had my tongue, others chimed in according to their own particular areas of gift-edness and offered to contribute in a variety of ways. Some offered to organize people around each of the leaders of a strategic segment, some committed to making sure the communication was clear and aligned. Others said they would get people together who felt called to pray for these efforts, and still others said they would be involved in either teaching or putting together teams for the administrative details.

In the time it took to evaluate this man's idea as a team and gain consensus that this was indeed the best way to go, everyone fell into place according to his or her best contribution and just filled in the blanks. It really was a beautiful thing to watch, and if I hadn't been so focused on myself, I might have seen the beauty in it.

Fortunately, I recovered enough to save face and not say anything stupid before the meeting ended. The drive home was quiet. I was the only one in the car. But there was no shortage of conversation going on in my head. I was ashamed of all the internal positioning I had done, even though no one else knew about it. (I have been a Christian long enough to know how to sin on the inside.)

I felt like a child, wanting all the attention and the credit. Wanting my gifts to be given the number-one prize. Wanting everyone to be directed and led by me so that even their contribution could be directly tied to my efforts. I wanted everyone on that team to think I was indispensable and responsible.

That's the bad news. And I am embarrassed to put it into print. But unless I am terribly mistaken, I am not alone in having had those less-than-brilliant leadership moments.

Here's the good news. It didn't even take me the full drive home (only about three miles) to realize how ashamed I was of myself. At least I had had the good sense to keep my mouth shut, or maybe it was just my good fortune that this all unfolded so rapidly I didn't have time to make a fool of myself. I was the only one who knew. But I did know. And once I was able to admit, to God and myself, how immature my reactions were, I was able to start moving past them. I was able to see what happened in that meeting as the great thing that it was. I was able to applaud this man's contribution and subsequently the contributions of so many others who rapidly got on board. I was able to be grateful for the team that was coming together in spite of me. I was freed from the terrible burden of feeling that everything was dependent on me, which is too much weight for any one person, really.

Getting me out of the way of my own team was one

of the best things that ever happened. Equally valuing and needing the various contributions each person had to bring was life giving and put us on the right path to solving our problem. Months later, I did admit what had been going on deep inside me that night. That kind of vulnerability is good for leaders. Difficult but good.

Turns out, everyone on my team had experienced similar feelings at one time or another. Whaddya know?

When we free ourselves up from evaluating and weighing and comparing everyone's contributions, remarkable things happen. It is easy, especially in churches, to put the blue ribbons on people with obvious up-front gifts—the teachers and leaders and singers. Their giftedness puts them in the spotlight in a way that almost inevitably leads to them getting more attention than they deserve.

When we free ourselves up from evaluating and weighing and comparing everyone's contributions, remarkable things happen.

But as we all know, there are some things that even a sermon or a song cannot do.

For seven of the nine years that John and I lived in Chicago, we worked on inviting our neighbors, Neil and Pat Benson, to church. Neil and Pat were great neighbors, the kind who are pleasant every time you interact with them and whose yard is a pleasure to look at. They were both schoolteachers in the local district, had no children, and put their Christmas tree up every year by Halloween.

So although I'm telling the truth when I say they were pleasant, I will admit that both their yard and their Christmas tree made me feel inferior. I still liked them, and we had a cordial relationship with them. We tried every which way we knew to get them to accept our invitation to come to church with us.

"Hey Bensons! John is preaching this weekend at our church, and we'd love to have you come with us."

Hmmm . . . we think we have to clip our toenails that day, but thanks for asking. And then that strained smile, with the subtext of "please don't ask again."

Undeterred: "Hey, Bensons, I am preaching this weekend. What do you say you come and then we all go out for lunch afterward?"

Wow, thanks for asking, really. We'll be grading papers, I'm sure.

The kids singing in a choir, Christmas Eve, nothing. So after a while, we just stopped asking. And actually, I think it was the right thing to do. It was getting a bit embarrassing.

Imagine my surprise when one bright spring day while I was standing out in the yard, Neil came bouncing over to inquire what time the Sunday services were, and informed me that he and Pat would love to come to church.

Huh?

He told me about a teacher's assistant who worked at their school. She was a single mom with three young children whose husband had recently and quite suddenly died. She had no car and struggled to make ends meet on a teacher's assistant's salary. Both Neil and Pat liked this woman a great deal.

Then they discovered that someone had given her—as in, no charge—a car. A used one, but solid, reliable transportation nonetheless. And that someone represented a ministry from our church that had been started by a guy whose life had been changed by Christ.

Here's the short but wonderful version of his story: This guy had started coming to Willow Creek when his life had hit the skids. His marriage and his job were in shambles. He was struggling with addictions that were seriously interfering with his life. And in that condition, he came to church.

After a period of some months, he understood the salvation of Jesus in that deep way that someone who is desperate understands. His life was truly and radically changed. His marriage survived and flourished, and with some help he wrestled free of his addictions. He regained his standing as a dad his kids could love, and he was incredibly changed and so incredibly grateful.

So one day he explained to our senior pastor that he had a strong desire to give back, and although he couldn't preach a sermon or sing, he had an idea. Spawned by gratitude and supported by his abilities as a mechanic, his idea was to start a "cars ministry" in which he and others would fix up and donate used cars, mostly to single moms.

And all the time that John and I had been inviting the Bensons to church, thinking they just needed to hear a great sermon or listen to beautiful soul-stirring music, their intersection with our church was with a mechanic. A mechanic, gifted by God, changed by God, and filled by God to overflowing.

The Bensons attended our church for the next two years, retired to Florida, and today are contributing members of a flourishing church in the land of sunshine.

One of the most powerful ways to motivate yourself as a leader is to remember back to a time when someone did it for you. Think back to a boss you had who took the time to notice the work you did, and let you know. That was probably a pretty powerful time.

I can still remember the first time this happened for me. I was twenty-two years old and working as a registered nurse. I was one of many new nurses in the orientation program at a large Catholic hospital that had a great reputation in our area. I felt a bit lost in the bigness and newness of it all. Although I had gone to college for five years to study nursing, now that I was working in a hospital for the first time, it seemed as though most of what I had learned was "theory." I quite literally found myself praying every day on my way to work: *Please don't let me kill anyone today.*

At the time, I was dating a guy who was attending an out-of-state school, and he was planning to come home on break just about the time I was scheduled to rotate from the day shift to my permanent shift: 3:00–11:30 p.m. I really wanted to stay on the day shift for two weeks longer. It would mean the difference between seeing my boyfriend and not seeing much of him at all. Although I was pretty motivated to ask, I was also terrified. I was new. No one knew me very well, and the director of nurses was a former nun. I don't know why that made her seem more formidable to me, but it did. That, and the fact that I had never even met her.

But I really wanted to see my boyfriend, so I rehearsed what I was going to say for days. I practiced presenting my case, not sure exactly how to ask for something after having only worked there for three months.

I picked the day and time I knew I would see the director walking in the halls. I asked the butterflies in my stomach to please take a break, and then, with all the courage I could muster, walked right up to her, put out my hand, and said, "You don't know who I am, but my name is Nancy Berg and . . ."

I kept talking, having memorized my request, which included good, solid reasons why this could work. But she interrupted me.

"I know who you are."

That's what she said to me. "I know who you are."

She then went on to say that she knew I was working on the medical-surgical floor, and that she had heard good things about my work. Eventually—perhaps out of pity (maybe the fact that she was an ex-nun was working in my favor)—she granted me the additional two weeks on the day shift, and I got to see my boyfriend.

There is power in paying attention.

I ended up marrying someone else, but I will never forget those five words: *I know who you are.*

There is power in paying attention. And a power is released in someone who knows he or she is being paid attention to.

Someone did it for you once. Now it's your turn.

Rubber Bands II

SO, BACK TO THE rubber band thing. Leadership is not an either/or, but rather a both/and. And as leaders, we constantly need to determine whether something is a problem to be solved or a tension to be managed. (One of my partners, David Ross, says this at nearly every off-site conference we conduct.)

Much of the frustration that leaders face comes from trying to solve what needs to be managed and trying to manage what needs to be solved. Being able to distinguish which areas need clarity and which areas will be ongoing tensions is a necessary skill. See, there it is already: the managing of the tension between clarity and tensions.

What needs what? If something can be solved, it is up to us to engage our teams in the problem-solving research and discussions that lead to solutions. But when we try to solve something that is really an ongoing tension, our frustration levels will inevitably rise, because tensions cannot and should not be resolved.

As leaders, we constantly need to determine whether something is a problem to be solved or a tension to be managed.

Working in the medical field a number of years ago, I had an employee who consistently did mediocre work and missed deadlines. I was a new young leader, and although I didn't realize it at the time, my need to have everyone like me still drove everything that I did. And even more than needing everyone to like me was probably an unspoken desire for everyone to think I was the best leader they had *ever* worked for.

(And even as I pounded that last sentence onto the page, I am aware of managing the tension of "did they work *for* me or *with* me?")

Anyway, I managed the tension of this guy's poor work for a long time—too long. But I had never done this before, and because he was quite a bit older than I was and had been with the organization years longer than I had, I didn't know what else to do. I talked with him, coached him on improvements, gave him deadlines, and checked in with him regularly. Occasionally I even covered for him while I was trying to get his work up to speed.

Then one day *my* boss sat down with me and talked to me about this employee's performance issues. I began with a long explanation of how I was managing this tension, to which he replied, "There is no tension. There is a problem here, and I have been waiting for you to solve it."

We talked at length about how long this had been going on with no signs of change, and how, mostly because of fear, I had put this issue into the managing or "developmental" category, when in reality it was neither of those things. It was an employee who was consistently underperforming in the basic areas of his job.

He was the first person I ever had to fire. Perhaps that is why the lesson is so memorable to me, even today.

Leaders know that tensions have to be managed all the time. Opposing forces can be found everywhere—in organizations, in churches, in people—and although both sides might have much to offer, either one can be destructive if one takes over without the other. Good leaders understand the need for equilibrium. Not balance, but equilibrium that is ever shifting.

Solving problems is much easier and more static. But managing tensions requires that you hold things open when what you would much prefer is closure; it is living in the foggy gray areas when what you want is clear black and white. And it is knowing what is needed when (because many times, closure and clarity are exactly what are needed!).

My son is a surfer. I, on the other hand, surf. There is a big difference, he tells me. I can get up on a long board if the waves are between one and three feet and the water temperature is hovering around eighty degrees. That last requirement is personal but nonnegotiable for me.

Johnny is a surfer. Given a wide berth of conditions, that boy can get up on his short board whether the waves are barreling or closing out, soupy or flat, gnarly or sweet. He can ride, cut back, top turn, and snap. He is beautiful to watch, fluid in his sport. He is passionate and persistent, two necessary traits in every surfer.

Surfing is this amazing intersection of controlled, known conditions and unpredictable, fickle forces. Days before Johnny chooses a time to go to one of his favorite surf spots, he is online assessing the weather conditions, checking out what is deteriorating and what is forming. He knows what the predicted wind patterns and directions will be and where the storms are. He watches storms that are generating destruction thousands of miles away because he knows they will also create glorious and perfectly shaped waves at our coast. He is aware of all the known factors: the direction the beach faces and the slope of the ocean floor at that location. He puts together what he knows with what is coming, and then he leaves room to factor in what he will find when he steps out of his car.

I have stood by him and watched as his eyes scan the surface of the water. He often stands in silence, the look on his face serious and considering.

Managing tensions is living in the foggy gray areas when what you want is clear black and white.

He is managing tensions. Really, the only immediate decision to be made is will he go in or won't he? Before and after that, it's still all about managing tensions. He will have to hold everything he knows right next to all that he doesn't know and live in that in-between place, where each wave is different and the wind can shift in a moment.

Many of the organizations I have worked in and that I work with now deal with the constant tension of infrastructure and innovation. You've got to have both. But they are not necessarily great roommates; they rarely get along and often compete.

Infrastructure versus innovation is not a problem to be solved, but rather a tension to be managed. And the struggle is not going to go away with a carefully timed decision. The interplay of the two, the necessity and the friction, are here to stay.

Our firm is currently working with a company that produces a lot of creative products in the form of TV commercials, radio spots, and print ads. Because what they produce demands innovative ideas, this company employs a boatload of creative people. But since it is a business, it also needs systems, procedures, administration, and detail-oriented people.

Meetings are a challenge. The systems people get frustrated when deadlines are missed, requests aren't filled out, and budgets aren't met. The creative people accuse the systems people of squelching their artistic inspiration with all these rules. And they remind the systems people that this is a *creative* business and that without the creative people, there would be no business.

Is this a problem to be solved or a tension to be managed?

In the same vein, think about the particular challenge that churches often face when it comes to passion and humility. Seemingly an endangered species, humble people rightly reflect the spirit of Christ in so many ways. Humility was portrayed clearly in the Gospels, and was such a defining characteristic that the New Testament writers were still recounting its virtues in Philippians and beyond. Humility puts us in right relationship to both God and to others; it sets the tone for our biblical community and allows us to serve and releases us from the need to compare and measure. In many ways, humility frees us up to be the best followers, the best leaders, and the most content children of God.

However (and that is a key word in the world of tensions), I have encountered people in churches who use this very wonderful word as a shield to hide behind as they work to avoid change, steer clear of truth, and relentlessly maintain the status quo, even when it renders them and the message of the gospel completely irrelevant to those who need it most. Humility can become a "get out of jail free" card that protects against accountability and honesty. I have seen it used as a shameless defense for protecting a personal viewpoint and as a weapon for destroying any sign of pride in a job well done.

So what is one to do with humility? Embrace it because it reflects Christ? That *can't* be the wrong answer. But what about all its misuses? Is humility the only thing we need; is it the end of the story? I don't think so. In order to truly understand humility, we must consider it in relation to other issues and values.

So let's add passion to the mix. Perhaps at first glance,

> **Humility frees us up to be the best followers, the best leaders, and the most content children of God.**

these two qualities appear to be somewhat opposite, competing even. Certainly there is some truth to that. In much of the work I have done in and with postmodern (or whatever the current language is) churches, I see a lot of passion. The people in these churches exude an energy that is palpable, a zeal that drives toward missional, and an enthusiasm for change and faith that restores hope. Passion breathes life into dusty organizations and keeps people motivated and engaged and creative.

I am not interested in living a life without passion. Put two people next to each other, one with passion and one without, and I'll choose passion every time. Okay, almost every time. People are attracted to it; they want to follow it. We need passion. The term may be overused and hackneyed and predictable seemingly to the point of irrelevance, but true passion is still vital to great leadership.

So how do we put these two together—passion and humility—in order to bring the best of both to the worlds we lead? Knowing all the good that humility can bring, while seeing with crystal clarity that it can also slip into a kind of low self-image and martyrdom that is not godly, how do we team it up with all the energy of passion, understanding that passion has the tendency to drift undetected into pride and arrogance? We must make humility and passion a both/and, not an either/or.

If you are looking for a direct answer and/or an equation for this, you have *so* bought the wrong book. Actually if you ever buy any book that promises to parse and spreadsheet this out for you, drop it and run. There is no clear-cut answer to this tension beyond this: *We must.*

We must figure out, perhaps in different ways every day, how to stand between differing forces and, as best we can, cull out the best and winnow out the worst.

We must have difficult conversations with others and take long, hard inward looks at our own motivations.

We must teach and talk about the two words (and all the "two words" that create tension) to define them and use them with wisdom.

We must release ourselves from the pressure to make decisions when the reality is that we are managing tensions.

When the occasion calls for it, we must celebrate that we (ourselves and our teams) have, as best we can, hit it about right.

Managing tensions isn't about compromise or consensus. It isn't about balance, which is too simply about finding the 50 percent middle ground and standing there. There is no tension in middle ground. Managing tensions is about finding the right place, given the particular set of circumstances and words, that gets the tension as right as we can, given that we are not perfect people. There are no perfect answers here, much like there are no perfect decisions. But that can never move us away from the tensions, only toward.

Toward the next wave and the next wave and the next. Each one different from the one before, each one wonderful in its own way.

defining *Moments*

LEADERS LIKE TO TALK about defining moments: critical times when we draw a line in the sand, put a stake in the ground. Defining moments are vivid times of commitment where direction is clarified, corners are turned, hills are taken. You can't always predict when they will occur, but it's this very element of surprise that adds to the drama.

We cannot live or lead without defining moments. We need them both individually and corporately. They write our history. They help us start new chapters, give us the courage to turn over new leaves, and breathe fresh wind into complacent and mediocre institutions. Defining moments are new beginnings and fresh starts.

They are all those things and at the same time, they are just moments. Anyone who has experienced a defining moment knows this. Some moments "take" and some don't, but the ones that count are those that somehow have the power to produce a new way of living.

Sometimes we mistakenly think that the power is in the defining moment itself. But the power is actually in the resolve following the moment, the momentum that emanates from it. It may be more accurate to say that the power is in the tandem of the two: the defining moment and the plan that follows. Defining moments are only as significant as the lifestyles they produce. If defining moments don't change things, they didn't define anything.

During my time in Axis, I experienced two particular defining moments, one that resulted in widespread lifestyle change, and one that didn't. Therefore one was truly a defining moment and the other wasn't, but I didn't know that at the time.

During the first few months in my leadership role at Axis, I joined regular attendees and people new to the ministry at a weekend retreat in Wisconsin. We started with a great teaching and worship session on Friday night, and then another similar session followed small-group experiences on Saturday morning. The afternoon was full of great outdoor free-time activities, and after dinner on Saturday evening, we had an evening worship service.

To say that the worship service was an event is an understatement. The band was amazing, and the energy in that room was just short of "rock concert." People wouldn't let the band finish, they kept clamoring for more, and as it got closer to midnight, I told my staff that I was going to bed and to be sure and wake me if they ended up having to call the police. Mostly that was a joke (although as my son constantly reminds me, in order to be a joke it needs to be funny), but that's how high the energy was.

Defining moments are only as significant as the lifestyles they produce.

The next morning I think most of the people were suffering from a "worship hangover," and breakfast attendance was sparse. By the time the final morning teaching session was ready to start, many people had told me how amazing the worship had been the night before.

I was sure the concert itself had been amazing, but I wondered if people were trying to make it into something it wasn't. When I spoke that morning I said this: "When the day comes that this Axis community—myself included—is giving at unbelievable levels, serving the poor with the same kind of energy I saw last night, and living deeply in authentic, Christ-centered, transformational relationship with one another, then I will believe that what we experienced last night was true worship."

But without all those things, our concert was nothing more than intentional frenzy that may have felt good in the moment but had no real, deep connection to the inner core of God. On the outside, the event had all the markings of a defining moment. But a closer look revealed that it was more like cotton candy: one bite and it dissolved. Nothing significant or lasting came from it.

(Now, as a side note, here is what I think is one of the most difficult things about leadership: I could have been wrong. It wouldn't have been the first time. My internal hunch could have been completely off. So saying what I said was a risk. But I couldn't shake the sense that something was off. Let me be even more honest. I wish it *had* been a defining moment. It would have been great for my reputation as a leader to have one so soon after starting.)

Fast-forward a little over a year later to a summer series we did in Axis called "21 C: How to Live an Authentic Faith in the 21st Century." We wanted to highlight people in their twenties and early thirties who were living out their faith in unique and authentic ways, and one of the people we invited to speak was Shane Claiborne.

Shane's talk was a defining moment that shifted Axis

into a lifestyle change. One hot August night, and the following morning, Shane talked to our community about what it meant to follow a Jesus who talked more about serving the poor than about prayer and what it means to be born again, put together.

In a winsome way that had more teeth than we even knew at the time, Shane spoke words that were prophetic. Through the teachings of Jesus and numerous Old Testament passages, he clarified for us the call for our discipleship to be infused with service to the underresourced. You can read a longer version of this story in *Looking for God*, but the end result of Shane's sermon was an altar of sorts, made up of more than seventeen hundred pairs of shoes, which were given to be distributed immediately to the homeless in Chicago.

Most of Axis left the services that weekend in bare feet.

But this time, Axis did the hard work of determining what would come after the bare feet. Our staff, as well as our key volunteer leaders, met together and talked and prayed about how we could keep this weekend from being just another moment. How could we build a lifestyle and a legacy around the holiness of what had just happened? We recognized how far away our ministry was from the vision that Shane had painted for us.

The beauty of what had happened led to pain. And

perhaps that is the key to moving from a defining moment to a lifestyle, this mixture of beauty and pain that prods us to movement and change. Heather, one of our Axis staff members, spent countless hours working with Axis people as well as community volunteers until she devised a rhythm of weekend serving opportunities.

Soon, the first weekend of every month, a team was heading into downtown Chicago and working with Bethel New Life, an organization that served the children of homeless families. The second weekend of every month, an Axis team was working with Feed-A-Neighbor, a downtown group that distributed food and clothing to the homeless. The third weekend of every month, a group from Axis was serving with Habitat for Humanity, doing construction on local sites. And the fourth weekend, a team was in the juvenile prison system. Every weekend, like clockwork. Regular teams were in place for each of those causes, and in addition any individual or home group could join up with these teams.

We began to make serving the underresourced *central* to our community. Not just a yearly event or a good idea. Not simply a thought with no reality, but a "set your watch by this" commitment. In addition, we began to ask all of our home group leaders in Axis to lead their groups to serve together regularly each quarter. Many of them chose one of these monthly ministries, but they were free to find their own if they wished.

We intentionally moved serving from the outer ring of influence more toward the center. Shane's sermon became more than the catalyst to remove the shoes from people's feet, a one-time deal. It spawned a reaction throughout our entire ministry that led us sweetly down the road of real discipleship.

The reciprocity was staggering. The serving, which was directing our resources and our efforts toward those in need, was only the beginning, as that God-given energy flowed back toward us from those we met in life-changing ways. In our weekend Axis services, we often told stories and showed pictures of children being helped, houses being built, and meals being distributed. We also told about the changes that were occurring in the lives of our Axis attendees who went for the sole purpose of giving and were stunned to see how much they gained in the process.

This will seem like a little thing, but we also rearranged our bulletin for the weekend services. We moved the order of the service over to the side, and used that front-and-center spot for ways people could connect into community groups or participate in weekend serving opportunities. We wanted even our bulletins to reflect the change and remind us of it weekly.

In our membership classes and our new leader training, we embedded this value of serving. We taught about it, told stories about it, and made it one of the functions of becoming a regular part of Axis. We just expected that people would join in. As much as reading the Bible, prayer, worshiping together at the weekend services, and being in community, service became a part of our fabric.

We contacted community leaders in neighboring Palatine, a fairly affluent community with a pocket of immigrants living in a small area that tilted the average income downward. They found ways for our Axis people to help teach ESL classes and to do after-school tutoring. We became partners with the Palatine Police Department in their summer efforts to keep kids out of gangs by sponsoring a day camp.

You couldn't come to Axis without understanding that an enormous part of how we were being transformed by Christ had to do with giving of ourselves to others, especially those in need. We took seriously and leveraged the gift that Shane had given us, to change us. The two-way street of serving did just what God had always intended: It changed us. It changed the shape and texture of our ministry, and over time, serving became part of our reputation. It began to define us, and it all started from that one moment.

There is a downside to defining moments that we can't ignore, however. While defining moments can propel us to great things, they can also become major obstacles to moving to the next levels. It's tempting to rest for too long on last year's defining moment—talking about it, replaying its details, telling stories about it, all the while becoming oblivious to the fact that we have stopped living it. Defining moments can be like quicksand that way. Before you know it you are underground, confused as to how you got there.

Our consulting team worked with a fabulous marketing agency for about a year. I often say that we get called in to work with an organization in three different scenarios: a group that is going through major upheaval; a group that is going through some transition and needs help; or a good team that simply wants to get better. All three have their own unique joys and challenges. This was definitely a good team that just wanted to get better, and those are fun clients to work with.

They were highly motivated, which came as no surprise since in their sleek, modern offices were tasteful displays of multiple awards they had won for their work in the industry. During the first few visits to their headquarters, one of my partners and I counted over thirty awards, plaques, and trophies from the last five years alone.

At one of our meetings with their executive team, a number of the team members were bemoaning the fact that they felt "stuck." They were certainly well respected and successful, but unlike the early days of the company, they lacked that hunger that had led them to enjoy their reputation for creativity and innovation.

As they went on talking about that, one of them reminisced, "Do you remember how we all felt the night we won that first award?" Those who had been there at the time nodded, as did the rest, who had heard about that experience many times. That night had been a defining moment for them. And for a while, it propelled them to great heights. But somewhere along the way . . .

As we talked about that defining moment, someone had an idea. I think a really great idea. In two days they would be having their monthly all-staff meeting. In preparation for that early morning meeting, what if they decided to go in and remove all the awards? What if when the staff arrived for the meeting, it looked like a burglar had stolen all of their awards—representations of all their defining moments?

We could hardly control the rest of the meeting. The energy that emanated from that one idea was unbelievable! The team talked for nearly an hour, imagining the response as well as planning what the meeting would be like after that. The ideas tumbled out, and sixty minutes later they had, at least on paper, the makings for another defining moment.

Sure enough, the meeting was everything they thought it would be, and more. The buzz in the offices was deafening, and by the time everyone had walked through the building and gathered in the large meeting room, it took them nearly five minutes just to get people quiet enough to get started.

After a great introduction by the leader, the staff was divided into fifteen or so smaller groups. One person from the leadership team sat with each of the groups, and for the next sixty minutes plus, they discussed how each person reacted when he or she saw that the awards were missing. Interestingly, something else emerged clearly in each of the groups. Nearly everyone in the company shared the same frustration that the leadership team had been expressing just days before. Those who had been there at the beginning missed the energy and excitement and productivity from those early days. Those who had only been there long enough to have heard the stories wondered if those stories would only be in the past.

The meeting allowed for a release and an unleashing of ideas, hope, desire, and commitment that had been simmering just below the surface, but took a "burglary" to tap into. That day, another defining moment occurred. And after the initial group work, another idea emerged. Those groups spent the final few minutes of the meeting writing out on colorful poster boards all the words that described what had won those awards.

Then, they took eight-by-eight-inch poster boards and placed them on small stands to hold them upright. With words like *whatever it takes, bold, relevant, inspiring,* and *What's our next award?* each stand was placed into the spot where just yesterday an award had stood.

When the group had come up with the original idea to remove the awards, they had planned on replacing them after the all-staff meeting. Unanimously and vigorously, however, the staff overwhelming chose to leave those words in place of the awards and only to take them down as they were replaced by new awards, which they were determined to win.

Now, the point of this story isn't simply about winning awards. It is about keeping people motivated, tapping deeply into that God-given desire and ability to create and innovate. How do we as leaders leverage defining moments for momentum? How do we recognize the signs of stagnation or decline, and do the work of leadership in reminding people what a great thing it is to work, to strive, to generate, and to build?

How do we learn to use the right touch and not to pile up relentless requirements for work that makes the soul weary? How do we clarify that continual call for people to give their best in such a way that stimulates ideas and moves us to new levels? How do we create an environment where everyone knows that no matter how great the past was, it will never compare to the future?

As leaders, we need to answer these questions. And perhaps, in doing so, we'll experience the most defining moment of all.

A final thought on defining moments and the momentum they should

There is often an enormous disconnect between the vision of an organization and the events that make up the daily calendar pages of the organization's leaders.

create: There is often an enormous disconnect between the vision of an organization and the events that make up the daily calendar pages of the organization's leaders. While vision can be a defining moment in an organization, often day-to-day responsibilities seem to have no connection to the realization of that vision. This inevitably leads to discouragement for leaders, teams, and organizations.

I know this well, not only because I have encountered the problem many times in coaching others, but also because it was pointed out to me during my time as a leader in the health care industry. I had a boss who was great at regularly sitting me down and going over my daily schedule to see if it aligned with my goals and the vision of the department. Too often, it did not.

His gentle question, "How will these activities result in the goals we have set?" was annoying but clarifying. I guess I just thought the vision fairy was going to come along and produce the vision while I engaged in activities that had no connection. I hate it when I am wrong.

However, a simple exercise both for individuals and for teams is to "audit" each other's calendars from time to time. Just have a simple discussion about what you are doing and why, and then speak about each other's choices, paying particular attention to the question "Does this activity move us toward our vision?"

"Does this activity move us toward our vision?"

With that simple question, my boss was able to help me use that as a grid for how I filled my days. Up to that point, I had always felt busy but not always effective. And that is a frustrating feeling: overworked but underchallenged, spinning wheels with little to show for it. With such a little shift, I was much better able to make good decisions about what I said yes to and what I said no to. No small feat.

Spending our yeses on activities that create movement

toward the vision is very inspiring because we can see the progress. When I started leading Axis, my boss gave me a handwritten half sheet of paper with three simple goals on it. I carried that paper inside my calendar for five years. It was my compass. I can't do twenty things well. I'm not even sure I can do six things well.

But three? Now I have a fighting chance.

bad person . . .
bad fit . . .
Big Difference

SO, I DIDN'T ACTUALLY get fired, but if it had been anything more than a two-week temporary job, I would have.

I should have.

During my sophomore year in college, a friend asked if I would fill in for her for a month while she and her husband went to visit family. She did administrative work for a company that developed the plastic coating for the insides of dishwashers.

Sounded fascinating.

I wanted to help out a friend.

How hard could it be?

It was a disaster. No, let's put it more honestly . . . *I* was a disaster. Some people are really gifted for administrative, detailed, and orderly work. Some are not. Who knew it could be so difficult?

Well, pretty soon I knew, and not long after that, the boss and others on the team knew. I remember sitting in that office, typing on carbon triplicates. Some of you who are younger will have absolutely no idea what a carbon triplicate is, but suffice it to say that any typing mistake took an act of Congress to correct. This was before the days of the backspace key for easily correcting mistakes. In those days, your mistakes were rather permanent, changed only with copious amounts of Wite-Out on each of the four carbon copies, leaving a reminder of your errors.

Every day I left the office with my purse *stuffed* full of mistyped carbon forms. My purse was only full after I had surreptitiously packed the restroom trash can, being careful to lay paper towels over the top so no one could see what I had put in there. I folded a few into my pants pocket and found a drawer that no one was using and made it my personal hiding place.

What took my friend minutes to type—with no errors—took me hours, and I am not exaggerating. I couldn't for the life of me figure out the filing system. The questions that people asked when they called in seemed to be in another language. I began to understand that I had vastly underestimated the complexity of the world of heat-resistant plastic coating.

I was so grateful that it was a slow month; I wouldn't have lasted two days if it hadn't been. That said, I lasted two weeks. Fortunately the boss was a big fan of my friend, and her job remained hers even though I didn't work the last two weeks. I think the way he put it was, "You know, Rob and Susan have some extra time these next two weeks, and I really think they can handle this."

I had become an obstacle to the business. (I still wonder if some units actually made it to their correct destination or are sitting in some cargo hold in East Asia.) And the leader had the courage to do something about it. I am pretty sure I heard a collective sigh of relief from the team as I left.

There is a big difference between a bad fit and a bad person. Leadership is about having the courage to make that distinction. Too often, we hide behind the belief that someone is a bad person, when the reality is, he or she is simply a bad fit. Many organizations and certainly many churches have allowed people to remain in positions (paid or volunteer) for which they are poorly suited. Everyone suffers when that happens.

The organization suffers. When someone is in the wrong position, vision, strategy, and results usually suffer.

The church or the ministry department or the business fails to live up to its God-given potential. The organization is crippled in its efforts to be all that it could be. That is not God's design for a church or an organization.

Individuals suffer. When a person is not well suited to his or her role, the people who work with and for that person inevitably languish in some regard. They either fail to get the support, recognition, or resources they need to do their jobs, or they are neglected in areas of discipleship and growth.

It is one of the fundamental jobs of a leader to make sure that the right people are in the right positions in an organization. Leaders who take action and initiative to make sure this is the case engender trust. Those who don't, cultivate cynicism and mistrust.

Certainly, systems can provide an infrastructure to support the alignment of the right people in the right positions. Things like hiring according to job descriptions and giftedness, 360-degree reviews, performance feedback, and one-on-ones are all necessary to accomplish this.

But the right person in the right position is more than a systems issue. Out in front of the systems must be the willingness to intercept entropy at its earliest signs, the courage to have difficult conversations, and the ability to set deadlines for resolution. A leader's observations and questions for a person who may not be the greatest fit for a position will help move this process along in healthy ways. The bad fit may be in areas of character or competency or both.

To overcome the bad-fit syndrome that plagues so many organizations, you need to tackle it from two directions. First, you will need to start right where you are, taking a look at those who might possibly be in the category of bad fit. You will need to find out if that is the case, and then lead those people through a process that either shifts them into a position more suited to their abilities and strengths, or moves them out of the organization in fair and honoring ways.

Second, you must take a look at the "on-ramp" in your organization: hiring. How well does your company do at the very beginning of the process to make sure that the fit is strong? This goes to issues of knowing what your values are and asking questions in an interview setting that check for alignment with those values. Do you allow a wide variety of people within your organization to participate in interviews so that you have a great cross section of opinions? Do you consistently call a candidate's references to be sure you get a fully orbed picture of his or her track record? This is not an issue of "good people"; it's more complicated than that. There are good people in every organization. This is an issue of finding good people with excellent abilities in the area for which they are being hired.

For many of my years in leadership, I seemed able to hire well in most areas—except for administrative assistants. I'm not sure exactly what the problem was, but I think one of them was that I vastly underestimated what it took to do that job well. I didn't realize that, like any other job, the skills needed to do this role required specific and unique abilities. Embarrassingly, I think I figured that anyone could do it. The obvious irony here was that I sure couldn't.

So I hired a great woman as the key administrative assistant for our department. Never mind that she was basically an artist. She was a good person. A *really* good person: likeable and fun, filled with great energy, helpful. Those are all significant qualities, but the one thing she couldn't do was administrate.

Details got overlooked, balls were dropped, and follow-through was poor. Our work was suffering and people were getting frustrated. But every time she would bounce into my office with her notepad, I found myself fooled by her earnestness, and I would think, *Okay, this will be fine.* And then it wasn't.

One day in my office, after we finished going over a long list of things she would need to redo, I just stopped. I looked her in the eyes and said as kindly as I could, "This isn't working, is it?"

And then I didn't say anything else. Her eyes filled up with tears and they started spilling down her face. Without saying anything, she just shook her head.

After a few moments I said, "I think you go home every night resolving to do better tomorrow. But I don't know how good it is for you to keep trying harder at something you aren't good at, all the while not doing the things you are good at."

She listened and nodded. Then the words just came pouring out of her. She had been miserable. She was trying *so* hard. She felt terrible about not doing a good job; it wasn't like this was a secret she didn't know. She knew very well how poorly she was doing, and she hated it. She thought that trying harder might help.

But you see, she was an artist, and artists don't make the greatest administrative assistants. Certainly there may be exceptions, but she wasn't one of them.

And you know how easy it is to get frustrated with someone who isn't doing a good job? She was even more frustrated than I was—with herself. And honestly, as a leader, I had to admit that I had let her down. After our conversation I felt terrible, realizing how keeping her in that position had done her a terrible disservice. I owed her more than that.

As we've already seen, one of the most significant jobs a

leader must do is to get to know his or her people, and out of that knowing, to be sure they are positioned according to their levels of character, competency, and energy. This woman and I had a wonderful conversation after the tears, and I pretty quickly moved her off staff. She has now written a number of best-selling novels and has been very successful in her life's work—once she was positioned to do what she does best.

This process takes time, and that's why one of the most important things to do is to work on finding the right fit during the hiring process. It's *a lot* easier to increase your success rate that way. Having to deal with people who are already in the wrong position is a lot more difficult and time consuming than it is to fill the position well in the first place.

When the wrong person is in the wrong position, the cost to the organization, in terms of morale and security, is high. So a leader has to be committed to that process. Max DePree often talks about leadership in terms of obligation—what we owe.

Leaders tend to have strong personalities, and strong personalities don't often like to think in terms of obligations. But there it is. Leaders are obligated. It is inherent in leadership. We are obligated to many things, not the least of which are clarity, expectations, feedback, and follow-up. We owe it to those we lead—not to mention the organizations in which we do that leading—to make accurate observations of their abilities and gifts and engage in honest conversations about their performance.

Leaders are obligated to many things, not the least of which are clarity, expectations, feedback, and follow-up.

Time consuming, difficult, and necessary.

Duty bound and obliged.

A few years back, one of my associate directors came into my office and made an observation. He laughed and said, "I've been watching you, and do you know that when you have someone on our staff who is a poor fit, or for one reason or another isn't working out, you ask them to read *Let Your Life Speak* by Parker Palmer? And if we have someone who is a great fit but might be contemplating a move, you ask them to read *Finding Contentment* by Neil Warren?"

Honestly, I hadn't noticed. Funny how the subconscious works sometimes. But the more I thought about it, the more I realized he was right.

We had a guy on our staff who was a terrific guy. Good person. And when he was first hired, he did a great job. But over time, he had either outgrown his job or he needed more challenge than we could at that point provide for him. Either way, things had shifted. He started coming late to meetings and staring at his computer during them. (Don't even get me started on that one!) Generally, he was doing a pretty mediocre job all around.

But he had been with us long enough that I wanted to give him the benefit of the doubt. I wanted to give him more time and understanding. I waited six months before having a direct conversation about the entropy I was seeing. That was five months and twenty-one days too long.

I was obligated to have that difficult conversation with him at the first sign of entropy. Here's the deal: Probably about eleven times out of ten, the answer to your most burning leadership issue is to *have the conversation*.

I know, I wish it was a different answer too. But it's not, so we might as well start practicing now.

When a conversation is going to be difficult, or when I'm not really sure what is actually going on or what the core issue might be, I have always found it helpful to start out with observations and questions. Save the direct statements for when there is unhealthy resistance or a blatant refusal to see the truth. Observations are not judgments, and they provide common ground for understanding. Observations imply that this is simply something you are seeing from an outside perspective

Have the conversation.

and that you acknowledge there may be something you are missing or are not understanding correctly. Observations leave room for explanations that will completely resolve everything.

Questions imply the need for more information. Now of course you can ask a question that isn't really a question, but rather a statement or an accusation. Those are not the kind of questions I am talking about. Real questions, the kind that help you to get an accurate picture of the situation and/or realize you need to talk to other people, help you to fill in the blanks and cross-check. At the very least, questions help you to start the conversation out on a level playing field.

And if it turns out you are on to something, you have started the conversation in a way that hopefully will position you to move toward resolution. These difficult conversations will have give and take, truth and grace, embarrassment and hope. You will have to listen, speak with boldness, forgive, understand, hold accountable, and ask for apologies. And then, most likely, you'll have to have more conversations before it is all over. If your response to all of this is "I don't have time for this," you are neglecting the obligations of leadership. Sorry to have to be the one to say it. I didn't like it the first time I heard it either.

Another thing these kind of conversations do is to create leaders who know what is going on in their organizations and allow everyone in the organization to know that they know. So many leaders are clueless about so many important things—not micromanaging kinds of things, but things like recognizing and responding to bad attitudes, poor work ethics, excuse making, blame shifting, underperformance, cynicism, and lack of results. The conversation at least implies that this is *not* okay.

One other type of bad fit that can affect an organization is the employee who holds everyone else hostage—the diva, the rock star. Got a name that's already popped up in your head? Certain people, often very gifted people, refuse to be team players. They do what they want, when they want. Their area is clearly the only area they care about, and everyone knows it. When their area is a central engine to the organization, the problem is magnified even more.

It is dangerous to allow any one person to wield that much power, and therefore that much energy, in the organization. As soon as you, the leader, have convinced yourself that without Lisa or Eric the organization would have to shut its doors, you have positioned Lisa and/or Eric to make your life miserable. And the other members of the team get smaller as they come to understand that they don't matter as much.

Don't get me wrong, we need rock stars. But we need them to figure out how to be team players as well.

Once you have all of these conversations going, you must go back to the beginning with your leadership team and have a robust discussion about what your values are, how you are all living them out, and the best way to craft interview questions that allow you to find someone who fits those values.

I know a guy who recently started a new job at a great, well-known organization. His second day on the job, he found a lovely glass pyramid on his desk. The person who was taking him through the group orientation explained that the pyramid was engraved with the company's vision and mission statement, as well as its corporate values. My friend quickly put his hand over the words and asked the guy, "What are the values?"

The trainer couldn't recite them and was obviously frustrated and embarrassed. Maybe it wasn't the best thing for my friend to do his second day at work. But he ended up leaving after eighteen months anyway; he found that the organization was not at all aligned with its values, and the only time he ever heard them referred to was during orientation.

Patrick Lencioni has written a great article about this very thing in *Harvard Business Review*, "Make Your Values

Mean Something." (And after you've read that, please read *everything* Patrick has ever written. And no, I don't make a dime off of any of that!)

Start working right now with your existing employees and/or volunteers to make sure everyone is a good fit. And at the same time, start to craft a hiring process that increases the number of great-fit people you bring on. This dual process can take a lot of time, but the rewards that you will reap at the end are well worth it. Imagine your organization full of employees who are deeply engaged in, passionate about, and greatly gifted for what they do.

It's the difference between using a bit and bridle to steer a wild horse and lighting a fire to get a mule moving. I have been a bad fit in a number of organizations. The plastic coating company was just one example. I was miserable. I tried really hard. I slacked off and wasted time. I went home feeling guilty, and then came to work the next morning with resolve that wore off before the first coffee break. I had no sense of accomplishment. I certainly wasn't adding value to the organization.

> **It's the difference between using a bit and bridle to steer a wild horse and lighting a fire to get a mule moving.**

Not good for me, not good for them.

The best leaders talked to me about it. The worst got angry or avoided me. The very worst didn't even know.

When an organization is relentless in its pursuit of people who are the right fit, it flourishes. No trash cans full of mistyped forms. As leaders, we owe that to the people and organizations we lead.

Teamwork Is a Strategy,

not a slogan*

A LOT OF LEADERSHIP writing has been done in the past decade about the power of teams. Since I believe so deeply in teams, I have read much of what has been written, and to be honest, most of it is really, really good. Which makes me wonder, why it is that I so rarely encounter really great teams?

Of course, some of that might be because my organization often works with teams in crisis or transition. But we also work with good teams that just want to get better. And even the good teams seem so plagued with divisive and draining issues that they aren't working anywhere

* with thanks to Patrick Lencioni

near their potential. Beyond those we work with, I've also talked with a lot of people who lead teams or are on teams, and rarely do I hear descriptions of stellar experiences or stories of teams that are both a pleasure to be a part of and known for results.

Of course, there are exceptions. On a recent school holiday, I made plans to meet with a friend and her kids for coffee (juice for the kids). When she arrived at the coffee shop, she immediately began talking in animated expressions about the great team meeting she had just come from.

"I thought you took the day off to be with the kids," I said.

"Oh, I did," she said. "The kids played in the board-room while we had our meeting. I wouldn't miss these regular Monday meetings unless it was an emergency. We always have such great discussions and updates about our projects. We're really moving some exciting projects forward, and we all know that we are better people when we get around each other."

That was a pretty staggering statement.

So how do you create, develop, and maintain a great team that isn't just about buzzwords but truly is the real deal? How do you use teamwork to your competitive advantage as a part of your leadership strategy? How do you live out the conviction that your organization and the people in it will be better as the result of being led by teams?

Create. One of the most significant jobs you have as a leader is the creation of your team. That means you come to work every day and you think about your team. Even with all the other things you have to do, you work hard to keep the formation and development of your team on the front burner at all times. When we commit to a leadership strategy, it drives our thinking, our meetings, and our decisions. That's easy to see when the strategy involves a direction in which we are heading, but it's perhaps a little less obvious when it is about the team that we work with every day. But if we don't make the team a priority, the breakdown begins and teamwork gets left in the heap of yesterday's buzzwords.

We need to take seriously the people who are on our teams. That sounds obvious, doesn't it? And it is, but rarely do I come across a team that doesn't include at least one member who probably shouldn't be there.

Do you have the right people on your team? That is not a vague, general question, but rather, it is one that you need to ask specifically in regards to each person: *Given what I need from this person, is he or she a good fit? Why or why not?*

Most of us are afraid to ask that question because any answer less than a resounding yes brings with it clear implications. We either need to work on developing those who don't fit, or we need to release them. Yep, that releasing part, that's hard. But while we might not admit it, it is even more difficult to have the wrong person on a team for years and years.

As we have already talked about, there is a *big* difference between a bad fit and a bad person. Every once in a while, we have to move people off the team because their character and morality is simply so off that they do not lead through the lens of values and have become an obstacle to great leadership.

In 2007, Internet giant Yahoo! was brought before Congress for providing China's government with confidential information belonging to a Chinese journalist. I read an article about the hearings, in which California Representative Tom Lantos made this great statement: "Much of this testimony reveals that while technologically and financially you are giants, morally you are pygmies." It really is possible to lead successfully but not lead well. That is a critical distinction for leaders to make.

Leaders who take action and initiative to make sure the right people are in the right places engender trust. Those who don't, create cynicism and mistrust.

Development is a great and necessary first step, and sometimes that is the ticket. But it's easy to hide behind "development" in order to avoiding the difficult conversations that could bring clarity to the problem.

And when the emerging clarity is that you need to move someone off the team, don't let avoidance set in. We will never move forward in the way we are hoping without the right people on the team—the right people in terms

It really is possible to lead successfully but not lead well.

of integrity, in terms of giftedness, in terms of energy, in terms of initiative, in terms of drive, and in terms of team-player mentality. You get to decide what the "right people" list looks like, but you need a list.

We worked with a really good leader recently. Every time we interacted with him, we were impressed by so many of his strong leadership qualities. He had integrity, vision, and drive. He articulated to his team what he appreciated about each of them, as well as a simple developmental plan designed to stretch them. He paid well and led dynamic meetings, and the company was succeeding in pretty fundamental ways.

But he had the wrong team. He had gathered this group around himself five years back when the company was just getting started. But the more we worked with them, the clearer it became that this one man carried the weight of the leadership.

Don't get me wrong, they were all great people. We liked each one of them, and they were good managers and implementers as long as someone handed them the instructions. But this wasn't a leadership team, and if they wanted to get where they wanted to go in the future, they needed a leadership team.

This was a painful discovery. There was a lot about this team that was good: strong loyalty and a feeling of family—things they didn't want to lose. But as we worked together to clarify the difference between a leader and a manager, and to discover how a leadership team functions to drive an organization, it was painfully obvious that what had gotten them to this point wasn't strong enough to take them to the next level.

Develop. Sometimes what will get you to that next level is development. You have the right people, but you can see that they need growth and maturity within their giftedness.

Here is one of the things that I most deeply believe about leadership: Leadership is the promise of development. Whether it's stated or not, inherent in great leadership is the promise that as a result of being led by me, you will emerge more connected in your relationship to God and stronger in your gifted areas. If you are my leader, it is my right to expect that I will receive that from you. And not only that, but to expect that as my leader, you will be a primary source of my development.

Part of what it takes to be a developmental leader is curiosity, the kind of curiosity that makes you a student of the people you lead. How well do you know them? You need to know their stories if you want to build trust. You need to know their giftedness if you want to fan the flames of potential. What kind of training, conversation, and opportunity do they need (deserve) in order to grow in their ability to lead?

I recently met with a guy who is the head of the graphic and video design department of his company. He was lit up like a kid at Christmas because his budget had been recently approved and he was sitting in front of some state-of-the-art computer and video equipment.

"This is one of the reasons I love working here," he told me. "They keep me in some of the newest and most exciting technology. I just can't wait to get to work most days. In the evenings and on the weekends, I sometimes find myself thinking about new ideas, because the way they equip me is so motivating!"

Leadership is the promise of development.

Can you image, contextualized of course for different jobs and budgets, if all of our leaders felt this way?

When I was leading Axis, we often had great conversations about some of the more innovative or creative ways the gospel was being furthered in other ministries. Whenever I could, I asked members of my team, "Would you like to fly out there for a couple of days to see firsthand what that group is doing?"

These trips went a long way in developing my team and making them feel known. They always came back reenergized and excited to get back to work.

Maintain. Surely this is not an exciting word. In fact, maintaining is near the bottom of my list of both interests and giftedness. But people need care and tending. If you do all this work to attract and develop the right people, you also need to keep

> **If you have great people and a great environment, you will do great work.**

them connected, provide the feedback (especially the positive side for maintaining), and know what is going on in their lives outside of work. When we describe it that way, maintaining takes on a much more interesting definition, one that I find quite motivating.

I want to make sure people on my team are getting time off when they have worked more than usual. I want to creatively and effectively reward their efforts and celebrate their accomplishments with them. I want them to know I am noticing and paying attention, and that I am grateful and amazed by their contributions.

It's our job as leaders to cultivate the teams that we have created and are developing, and to provide conditions under which they will flourish, in many areas of their lives, not just leadership.

I want to run into more teams where people are energized by the results they are experiencing and fully connected to the people they work with. One leader I worked with recently said, "I think if you have great people and a great environment, you will do great work."

Maybe it's that simple.

the hardest person to *Lead*

IT DOESN'T TAKE LONG to realize that leadership is hard. You should be able to conjure up the names of at least five people who make that a true statement. All kinds of things make leadership difficult, but certain people are one of those things.

As the picture of those certain people comes to mind, take a minute to let that picture fade. Because of all the difficult people you will lead, the hardest person to lead will be yourself.

Call it whatever you want—the discipline of a leader, self-leadership, managing yourself—you've got your work cut out for you. Many of my former bosses will laugh aloud when they read this part. They will find it humorous that I am writing about self-leadership, and perhaps be relieved that I am finally getting it.

The journey of leadership is as much inward as it is outward. Leadership, done well, will continually be a force that drives you back into the center of yourself to find out what you are really made of. Great leadership occurs when you understand your own motives, your "dark side," what you want to misrepresent in order to look better than you really are.

> **Leadership, done well, will continually be a force that drives you back into the center of yourself to find out what you are really made of.**

One of the things I believe deeply is this: Leaders ought to be the most self-aware people in the room. Sure, who doesn't agree with that? Especially if I clarify that I am not talking about a narcissistic self-awareness. You know the kind: the people who only know two pronouns: *I* and *me.* No, not that kind of self-awareness.

I'm talking about the kind of self-awareness that makes you comfortable in your own skin. You know who you are and who you aren't. You lean into and lead out of your strengths. You have words for your brokenness, and while you may wish you had none, you know that you do and you know what they are. And you know that other people know. You wouldn't have it any other way.

People like that are lovely, aren't they? Strong and lovely.

When I was in my early twenties, there was a woman in our church like that. She was probably in her midforties, and I remember thinking that if God would let me live that long (I was sure she was near death, at her age), I would love to be just like her.

Good leaders lead well for the sake of themselves. We must possess a deep level of insight into who we are and why. In order to lead out of good motives, we need to be aware of our blind spots and lead for the good of others rather than filling some void in ourselves.

And good leaders lead well for the sake of others. A significant part of leadership is helping others function out of that centered place, and the best person to lead us there is someone who has already traveled that difficult road.

This brings me to the tough part. Why is it that so many leaders lack self-awareness? Because it's hard. Some of the hardest work you will ever do. The difficult inner journey.

And because it's hard, and because it's on the inside, sometimes we just don't do it. It's easier to simply cover it up with outside stuff that looks impressive, burying the soul under a heap of life's rubble. You, me, and Dorian Gray.

Here's the paragraph where I write what you already know: Eventually, avoidance will catch up with you, so you might as well pay attention now. If you don't, it's only a matter of time before you will be exposed for the empty, hollow shell that you are. The outside will get stripped away and the big reveal will show that your motives and ego were bigger than your leadership. And you will crumble.

Maybe.

Sure, that's possible, and we've all been spectators of that unraveling without having to buy any tickets. But it is also possible to keep on living and leading out of a hollow and selfish center, and do it until you die.

There are a lot of reasons to lead yourself well: so you don't get caught, so your influence won't disintegrate, so you won't lie on your deathbed with overwhelming regrets. But none of these are reason enough. Only authenticity will do.

Good leadership is about what is real and right. It is about God, and isn't He real and right?

My husband, John, once asked this question: Is the life you're inviting others into, the life you're leading?

I love that line because it speaks to authenticity and truth. Do I believe it?

It's such a simple truth. If I really believe that God's

way is best, I would be a fool to live any other way. And if I don't believe that, why in the world would I give myself to leading others to it?

Like so many things, self-awareness comes down to the bedrock of God. Can we trust Him? Is He good? Answer those two questions and you will be a long way down the road of that inner journey.

Leading yourself is largely about living a rhythm of life that renews the life of God in us. It's about doing what it takes to know God and enjoy Him and follow and trust Him. It's about being utterly convinced of His goodness. It's about passion and energy and joy that come out of that center.

Leadership that's built on the bedrock of God is about a lot more than "quiet

Good leadership is about what is real and right.

time." In fact, let me go out on a limb here. I think for many Christian leaders (whether in a church or an organization), one of the biggest detriments to their relationship with God is quiet time. Connecting to God in the same way, at the same time, every day can be a surefire way to squeeze the life of God right out of you.

Good leadership is about developing a rhythm of life, not an equation. I think setting aside some time to read the Bible, to pray, and to journal is a wonderful, life-giving practice. Sometimes. But I am talking about something much larger and more integrated than that single practice.

Over time, if we're not careful, ritualized quiet time can foster an external behavioral modification approach that leaves us smiling and praising God on the outside but distant and empty on the inside. External practices have never been the end goal. But because they are visible and measurable, we are often tempted to substitute them for the real thing.

In Isaiah 29:13, God registers His strong displeasure with His people: "These people come near to me with their mouth and honor me with their lips, but their hearts are far from me."

Ouch.

I *hate* it when He hits the nail on the head. I much prefer when He rails against somebody for doing something I don't struggle with. Then I can join in the amen chorus. Yeah, that's right . . . you tell 'em.

Good leadership is about developing a rhythm of life, not an equation.

But He goes on to further expand his gripe: "Their worship of me is made up only of rules taught by men." As if this message wasn't painful enough already. All right, all right, I get it.

There is a hauntingly strong parallel between this Old Testament passage and Matthew 23, where Jesus levels

His criticism at the Pharisees. Starting in verse twenty-five, Jesus tells them that their insides clearly don't match their outsides. He says they are like a cup that is clean on the outside but filthy on the inside.

It's easy to sit back with Jesus and point our fingers at those awful Pharisees. Those bad religious leaders. Then Jesus goes on to tell us what it is that makes the cup dirty: greed and self-indulgence. I sure wish He would have said murder and adultery, or at the very least, extortion and embezzlement.

But no, He goes with greed and self-indulgence. Two things that get Him so worked up that He accuses the Pharisees of hypocrisy. So close to home.

This rhythm of life with God that renews the life of God in us is about a whole lot more than a daily quiet time. It is about knowing and connecting with God in transformational ways. Ways that change us, release us, quiet us, engage us. Ways that utterly convince us of His goodness, ways that free us from fear and give us a lightness of spirit in the midst of the burden of leadership.

I live about twenty-five minutes from the Pacific Ocean. There are times when walking along that wild coastline centers me with God in deeper ways than any quiet time I have ever had. The sight and sound of water that has traveled for thousands of miles, releasing its energy onto the shore . . .

the enormous immenseness of the sea . . . the breeze, the smells . . . the dolphin slicing up through the water and a pelican diving down. The ocean has a bigness that envelops; it is still in motion even when I am away from it and have forgotten its power and majesty. I am no match for it, and yet I feel a sense of calm when I am present with it.

Some days this ocean is the nearest thing to God that I know.

Recently, John and I had lunch at a nearby Mexican restaurant. It is small and family owned, and festive inside. Just walking in the front door brings a smile to my face. We ordered, and within minutes, servers were placing plates of mouth-watering, beautiful food in front of us: grilled fish with mango/red pepper/cilantro salsa, green and red cabbage dressed in a light vinaigrette. Soft, warm flour tortillas with beans covered with a dusting of cheese. Three different kinds of salsa to add to the mix and a pico de gallo to kick it up a notch.

Looking at and eating that meal was a prayer. A reminder of a gratuitous God who is so full of goodness that mangoes and red snapper exist. A lesson in the abundant nature of God and His provision. A lesson in joy.

I know a lot of leaders who need all of those lessons and reminders.

I am one of them.

I want to lead out of a core in my being that is deeply connected to that God. I believe that if I grow a core like that, it's more likely that my motives for leading will be good ones. I believe it will cause my leadership to be more authentic and visionary. Only good things could come from working on a core like that.

Leading myself well and connecting deeply to God involves acts of serving that are outside the limelight: kindness to a harried busboy, patience with a slow driver, an extravagant tip for a waitress. These are responses that help me to remember that I am not the center of my or anyone else's leadership. They are responses that reflect what I believe to be true about God.

I remember a coaching session I had once with a pastor of a large church. After listening to him talk for a long time, I had one question for him: "When is the last time you picked up your own dry cleaning?"

I could tell by the expression on his face that he was quite confused, but I knew I was onto something. This man's leadership role had isolated him from everyday living to the point that he was almost completely devoid of understanding or compassion for people. Of course there was much more to it than that, but we decided that the best place to start might be by picking up his own dry cleaning from time to time.

Crossing paths with a wide variety of people is a good spiritual practice. Considering their stories and circumstances, their hardships and joys, can do much to center us strongly in God. When we move beyond the traditional quiet-time approach, we realize that all of life is spiritual formation.

The experiences, observations, and responses we have in life are the crucible for transformation. Interacting with God when we see a need, have a thought or a feeling, become aware of an opportunity—all become grounds for connecting with Him. The wrestling, the frustration, the submission, the cry for help—all these things shape our hearts, minds, and souls. They are all moments of invitation for God to enter our lives and change us.

Our brokenness becomes a place of spiritual formation. It's easy to avoid this brokenness by pleading for grace—or rather, "pseudo grace." We rename it and compare it with others, all in the hope that we'll be graded on a curve and found to be not as bad as someone else. But ironically, the very thing we shy away from has the capacity to bless us in amazing ways if we will just face it.

Two of the most powerful things that God offers us are His grace and His forgiveness. So rather than avoid our sin and brokenness, we need to name them. And then, those places can become the very places where Jesus appears, bringing with Him the cross and the empty tomb.

Sometimes, quiet time is nothing more than a rule by which we measure whether or not we are "good enough." But the point of the Cross is that there is no "good enough." There is nothing that you and I can bring that can restore our relationship with God.

Leaders who are appropriately connected to the reality of their brokenness and the gift of God's forgiveness are able to easily utter the words that build community: "I'm sorry." Great leaders say it authentically and often. It is impossible for people who sin to build relationships and not have to apologize on a regular basis. Too often, our pride has us choking on those two little words.

But deeply forgiven people are deeply grateful people. Jesus made this clear in His parable of the one who was forgiven much. Deeply forgiven people are capable of genuinely forgiving others.

Here is one final thought on leading yourself. There is a profound passage in John 16. In this Scripture, Jesus has made it clear to His disciples that His death is imminent. In addition, He has told them that in the face of that, they will soon abandon Him. "You will leave me all alone," He tells them. But in the next breath He says, "Yet I am not alone, for my Father is with me" (verse 32).

That description of a soul connected to God, even when everyone else is gone, is the bedrock of a life of faith. Are you living a rhythm of life that is weaving that in you?

Leaders often say that leadership is lonely. Jesus said that kind of aloneness makes you realize that God is always there. There is a difference between being left alone and being without a Presence.

There will come a day that isn't about your leadership at all, the day when you find that your final breath is near. That is the main point of self-leadership—a life spent fighting and connecting with God so that, in those last moments, you are not alone.

T-shirts, *Redux*

AT ITS HEART, VISION is about a journey we are taking together. The destination is motivating; we can hardly believe we might actually arrive someday. But in addition to that, we find that along the way we are changed. Vision is always about the "we" and the "I."

A powerful combination.

By myself, I cannot implement a systemic solution to extreme poverty, but with a group of like-minded and committed people, I can. By myself, I cannot change my character or spiritually form myself, but in community, I can.

A vision compels us to look at a brighter future, and it

insists that we be changed in the process. A vision isn't big enough if it leaves someone unscathed. Vision is challenging, both to the work we do and the people we are.

The job of a leader is to devise creative, compelling, and repetitive ways to communicate the vision to the people. Vision is simply the motivation, and motivation implies doing something. What we are going to do and how—now *that* gets everyone in the game.

Recently we did some follow-up work with a church that had just shut down for the weekend to engage everyone in serving opportunities throughout the community. They had been planning this weekend for months. They had researched and interviewed potential partner organizations they could join with for those two days in reaching out to the needy in their area.

They had communicated both the vision and the plan with the congregation for a few months prior to the actual weekend. People got excited to serve with their families or their home groups in the areas of elderly people, education, food banks, and shelters.

Various opportunities were available and people signed up for shifts to read to patients in nursing homes or to do manual labor at some of the area schools that were in desperate need of refurbishing. Slots were available for people to bring, stock, and distribute food items in three local food banks, and meal preparation and cleaning were needed at two nearby homeless shelters.

It was a bold step for the leaders to shut down the church on a Sunday. In fact, there was a bit of initial resistance to that. But when the vision was communicated, and pictures were shown and stories told about the need, eventually those complaints were replaced with sign-ups.

As the weekend got closer, the decision was made to have one Sunday evening service for anyone who wanted to share and reflect on the experience. I showed up to participate in that service and to do work with the staff team the next day, and I was overwhelmed by what I saw. On Sunday night, hundreds of church people, most of them still wearing work clothes, poured into the sanctuary. They should have been exhausted. They were dirty, and they didn't smell so great. They should have gone home, but I got the distinct impression that wild horses couldn't have kept them away.

The event had clearly tapped into something, something you rarely see even in a worship service.

As a leader, when you are able to drive down deep and get to the "I want" motivation, the organization becomes a perpetual-motion machine. It no longer requires as much of your own energy, because those around you have a zeal for the job. And that energy is enough to carry all of you collectively well into the future.

Vision needs to be nurtured, and the conversations that your team is having about the issue of vision are critical. I have a friend who is currently researching and writing a book on parenting. One of the most fascinating findings he has uncovered is this: As parents, if you and your spouse spend ten minutes a week talking about your children—what their current issues are, what you want to work with them on—you are in the top 0.2 percent of the population.

When you are able to drive down deep and get to the "I want" motivation, the organization becomes a perpetual-motion machine

I don't think it is much of a stretch to extrapolate that idea to leadership. If you are talking with the people on your team even once a month about the vision and their role in it, I think you are way ahead of most teams I encounter.

If you set aside one hour a month for a robust conversation with your leadership team about the vision and its current implications for each of you personally and for the organization as a whole, you're probably far beyond most others.

You want to grow your leadership team into a leadership community that stimulates growth in each member. If they are done well, the conversations you initiate, the debates you participate in, and the decisions you make all foster and fuel the vision. The vision continues to be a shared vision when everyone is invited to participate in talking about it and shaping it into the future.

In Axis, our vision was made up of three strategic components: creating vibrant, authentic community; helping our friends to discover Jesus; and serving those in need. As a team, we regularly got together to talk about these components.

Creating vibrant, authentic community sounds great, but it is really hard work, and we didn't want to lose sight of that or let it become an obstacle to our purpose. During these meetings, we invited each other into open and honest dialogue about the ways in which we were experiencing or not experiencing community. Sometimes our conversations were about ways in which we were failing to create biblical community, or ways in which it was breaking down within our organization. Other times, we talked about the rich and meaningful ways in which we saw our community growing.

Always, we asked ourselves this question: Are we as a team creating and experiencing the kind of community that we are hoping others in Axis will?

During one conversation where we were talking about helping our friends to discover Jesus, one of our staff members realized that working in ministry had isolated him from people who didn't know God. He knew that our vision included him, so he decided to do something about it.

In addition to his job with us, he took on a small part-time job at a local Starbucks. There he worked alongside people his age from different walks of life. He built friendships with them and found ways to serve them and know them.

If the vision doesn't cost us something, we aren't participating. Because of this guy's decision, the rest of us began to take our non-Christian friendships more seriously; rarely did a meeting go by when we weren't asking him how things were going at Starbucks.

Our leadership team didn't simply have the task of helping Axis serve the marginalized, however. We knew that *we* were called to be active participants in that lifestyle as well, so from time to time we talked about the ways in which we were actively serving the underresourced.

Much of the work of vision is planting seeds, ideas for doing things differently. Like seeds, much of the transformation happens slowly at first, beneath the surface. There is a dormancy period, where from every view it appears as though nothing is happening.

But nothing could be further from the truth. Here is where the persistence and patience of a leader is needed more than ever. *Patience* and *persistence* are not words that leaders normally gravitate toward. But they are critical, as are constant soil prepping, planting, watering, and feeding.

Ask any schoolteacher how often students have returned with the words "What you taught me really made such a difference in my life." Many teachers are taken by surprise when this first happens, because when the student was in the classroom, the teacher saw no indication that he or she was even listening.

The interesting thing about seeds is that they contain much of the energy and direction necessary for growth within themselves. Then they are buried underground, where much of the rest of what they need exists. And they lie there.

Sometimes there is absolutely no sign of growth for months. In fact, the ground looks exactly as it did the day you buried those little suckers.

And then one day, you see it. At first you have to blink, not sure if it is what you think it is, it is so small. But sure enough, there it is: a tiny little green shoot. And once it gets its head above ground, it makes up for lost time, growing so quickly you could swear you can see it getting taller almost daily.

It is there that we see that convergence of the seed, the soil, the depth of planting, the water, the sun, and time. Perfect conditions for growth.

Creating a leadership culture does much the same thing.

The vision, the values, the shared goals, the meetings, the conversations, the relationships . . . all these things work together to create a climate that supports and encourages growth.

And that climate also creates vibrancy and allows people to flourish in such a way that those things become characteristic of both the individuals and the organization.

Scot McKnight writes about the conditions under which people change. His conclusions are applicable here, in the context of vision and creating a leadership climate and culture.

The vision, the values, the shared goals, the meetings, the conversations, the relationships . . . all these things work together to create a climate that supports and encourages growth.

Scot says that people are most open to new information and to change when they are either on a quest or in a crisis. This is important information for leaders to use in shaping their teams.

I want people on my leadership team who are on a quest, people who are naturally curious and are drawn to the journey of transformation. People who aren't satisfied with the status quo or life as usual.

People who are on a quest ask questions. (I am sure there is an etymological connection here.) They humbly consider their sins and weaknesses as possible contributing factors to disagreements or relational breakdowns. They read and learn and apply. They are drawn to growth.

People who are on a quest are courageous. It is much easier to live "questless," taking the path of least resistance, but people who are on a quest are willing to live with discomfort and ambiguity, knowing that eventually those things will cause the seed to grow. People who are on a quest are transformed.

One of the most significant questions leaders can ask themselves is this: How do I create a culture that attracts people on a quest? In our meetings, in our one-on-ones, what am I doing to facilitate those qualities?

Good leaders ask a lot of questions. It's easy to think good leaders *answer* a lot of questions, but I don't think that's true. I remember one day sitting at my desk at work and being terribly frustrated about something. So I called Max DePree. I've found that to be one of my best strategies when I am frustrated.

After I explained the situation to him, Max said, "Nancy, you do know, don't you, that leaders are only right about 50 percent of the time?"

No, Max, I did not know that. Thanks for telling me *now*—where were you with that interesting little tidbit twenty years ago?

Fifty percent, is he kidding me? I had been operating

for years under the assumption that leaders need to be right at a 90 percent average or better. Ever felt relieved and confused at the same time?

Good leaders teach their teams to think. One of the strongest responses a leader can use is this: "I don't know; what do you think?" That question is an invitation to contribute, participate, choose, and direct. Giving people a choice honors their dignity as human beings. (That's another thing Max taught me; you honor the dignity in another person, you do not bestow it. I think that is very profound. We should all spend at least a full day thinking about that idea, as well as its implications.)

Giving people a choice encourages the quest. People on a quest have a much better chance of moving toward a vision than people who are not on a quest.

People on a quest often change other people. In Axis, we were challenged and changed by a person in our ministry (not on the leadership team) who was on a quest. His name was Quinn.

Quinn was about twenty-four when he started attending Axis. He was a bit different than the average Axis attendee in that he had already experienced a great deal of success in business at an early age. He drove a Mercedes-Benz, and I am pretty sure he was the only one in Axis who did. Yeah, take that to the bank.

Anyway, Quinn started attending Axis because some of his friends did, and they had told him about the pretty girls there. Sometimes you can't be too proud about what draws people to your ministry. So Quinn started coming to the services, hanging out with people afterward, even joining a home group.

People who are on a quest are transformed.

Interestingly Quinn was driven to find the answer to one question. He wasn't asking about redemption, the Cross, or even life after death. He simply wanted to know if these people who said they were Christ-followers actually tithed. He was really stuck on the 10 percent thing. And everywhere he went, Quinn asked that question.

After the Axis service, when everyone went out to Chili's or over to someone's home, Quinn grilled people: Do you really give 10 percent of your income to church? He didn't care about net or gross, he just couldn't believe anyone would believe so deeply in something that he or she would engage in this kind of giving.

At many of our Axis leadership meetings, someone would tell a Quinn story, about him attending an evangelism class (now that's hilarious, this seeker guy going to a Contagious Christian class, mostly to ask his question), or going to a party, drilling people with his question. Quinn was definitely on a quest.

Quinn's quest affected most of us on the leadership team. Stories of Quinn prompted discussions of our practice of giving and whether or not we did. Some who weren't regularly tithing began to do so as a result of our conversations.

Quinn encountered many people his own age, most of them making much less than he was, who could authentically and enthusiastically answer yes to his question, and follow it up with reasons why they gave. Somewhere in the middle of Quinn's quest, he met Jesus. Quests transform people.

Scot McKnight also says that people are open to change when they are in a crisis. For a team this could be a personal crisis or an organizational one. The bottom line is this: Often during a crisis, people are most open to new information and the possibility of change.

Leaders need to respond to both. A personal crisis in the life of one of your team members is an opportunity for you to move toward him or her. (Occasionally you might have a team member who is perpetually in crisis; that is not what I am talking about here. That is a huge issue that needs to be dealt with directly.)

I know of leaders who have helped a team member obtain a vehicle, find a counselor, and pay bills. The accessibility of a leader in times of personal crisis is a reflection of authenticity and care. By listening and asking questions, you can help the person in crisis to not be paralyzed or feel like a victim. It will also convey that you are not merely interested in the person for what he or she contributes at a work level, but as a person with a life—a person who from time to time has a crisis.

An organizational crisis becomes an opportunity for a team to rally together and debate and make decisions around the appropriate response and direction in the face of the problem. Crisis becomes the impetus for open and honest discussions on a team.

A quest, a crisis—seeds . . . buried, cultivated. A few questions, a little crisis—a lot of growth.

what you may not know about
Mongooses[*]

"IT IS THE HARDEST thing in the world to frighten a mongoose, because he is eaten up from nose to tail with curiosity." That's from *Rikki-Tikki-Tavi* in case you need to credit the source the next time you use that quote.

The best leaders I know display an uncommon confidence that reassures people. They are comfortable in their own skin and exude an indomitable spirit that inspires others. Interestingly, one of the things this confidence has at its core is an unceasing curiosity.

Deeply curious people put themselves in the posture of a learner almost all of the time. They are full of questions,

---

* Apparently the plural of mongoose is not mongeese.

always wanting to know more and constantly expanding their understanding of all kinds of subjects. They listen and absorb information, thoughts, and perspectives different from their own.

We often coach two very different kinds of leaders. The first is not curious and, I would say, is often driven by fear. Whenever observations and feedback are given, the uncurious leader responds with defensiveness and rationalizations. With these leaders there are no questions, only hurt silence, quiet passivity, or statements designed to protect themselves.

The second type of leader is curious. These leaders respond from a position of wanting to gather information and trying to understand. Whether it is negative feedback, a missed opportunity, or the future direction of the organization, this leader is interested and inquisitive, wondering not *if* this will be solved, but *how*.

So what is the connection between curiosity and fear? It seems that when one increases, the other decreases. Perhaps it is not a lack of curiosity that makes us fearful, but fear that prevents us from being curious. Or maybe it's the other way around. The good news is that without solving the riddle of the chicken and the egg, I think we can tackle it from either end.

Fear produces poor leadership and poor leadership produces bad organizations. You can smell fear when you walk into a building; it permeates the meeting rooms and the break areas. You can see it in the eyes and hear it in the voices. Fear makes us tentative; it causes us to hesitate and posture. Fear is exhausting, but those who are living in it feel as if it is their only choice.

So what is the connection between curiosity and fear? It seems that when one increases, the other decreases.

The politics of fear consume vast amounts of time that ought to be spent focusing on vision and strategy. Instead, we waste our most precious resources of time and talent on diffused energy and spinning wheels.

Fear causes us to make poor decisions and then to second-guess those decisions. It forces us to retreat into business-as-usual mode, keeping our heads down and choosing our battles. It makes us small and weary and on edge, with the crunching sound of eggshells always in our ears.

That's the bad news.

The good news is that leaders can do a lot to abolish a culture of fear within their organizations. Since many culture-shaping behaviors begin with the leader, good leaders always need to ask themselves what role they are playing in creating a climate of fear in their organizations.

It's often difficult and painful to trace fear back to its

roots; fear has *a lot* of sources. But at the risk of sounding therapeutic, let me just say this: Unless you are willing to go to the place where fear began, you won't have a lot of luck changing it.

And just to add to the complexity, a lot of leadership behavior that looks "non-fearful" is actually teeming with fear. Stuff like command and control, because-I-said-so, and rigid thinking. These things look different than slumped shoulders and averted eyes, but they are not.

Often the top leaders of an organization are the source of much of the fear. And sometimes it is their fault. Sometimes it is not. We worked with one organization where everyone on the leadership team seemed to be afraid of giving open, honest feedback to the leader. You know, the kind of feedback that can derail people and companies if it's not given.

Anyway, at every break—yes, every one—during the two-day off-site seminar, a different member of the team, or sometimes a small group of them banded together for support, would corner my partner or me and implore us to tell the leader some of the truth, even just a piece of it, that they were holding.

They had wild eyes that darted furtively back over their shoulders, scanning to make sure the leader didn't see them engaged in this stealth activity. They spoke in hushed tones and told us with assuredness that they were "not the only ones who feel this way."

"Everyone is afraid of him. No one can tell the truth; we get punished if we do." We heard it again and again.

And then, a funny thing happened. With some gentle coaching and setup from us, one person ventured out into the truth. Hesitatingly at first, but then emboldened by the sound of his own words, he continued.

Interestingly and surprisingly, the leader responded, "I was afraid that's what people might be thinking. I am so glad you said something. What can we do about that?"

He was afraid too. And glad that someone had the courage to speak the truth. And wondering if they could come up with a collaborative and right solution.

Now I'm not writing fairy-tale endings, but this really did happen. And because it did, the courage of one person to challenge the faulty mind-set of that team started ever so slowly to shift the culture of that company.

They had been so afraid, and so sure that their boss would react angrily to their speaking up, that they kept quiet. But here's the deal: Sometimes we are afraid of things that aren't scary. Sometimes it is *our* problem rather than the other person's. Sometimes we create a culture of fear all by ourselves.

Sometimes we project all of our own fears onto the leader,

and then criticize that leader for being scary. Kind of put that person between the rock and the hard place, don't we?

Strong leaders become Rorschach blots for our own fears. So although it may feel counterintuitive, sometimes the place to begin unraveling a culture of fear is with ourselves.

Perhaps the best question to help us do that is this: What am *I* afraid of? The answer to this will help create clarity, both about the worst thing that could happen and where our fears are rooted, internal or external. What personal issues of feeling abandoned, needing to please people, or lacking self-esteem might we be ignoring by claiming that someone else is causing the fear? And just by asking these questions rather than reacting defensively, we put ourselves in the curious world, where fear is diminished.

It's so much easier to blame our fear on someone else, especially our leader. She's getting paid more anyway, we tell ourselves. Might as well blame her. It is so much easier when the fault lies with another person, because then we don't have to do all that hard soul excavation, that heavy lifting.

Recently our firm worked with a very impressive organization. It was probably number two or three in a field that is technical enough that I'm not sure I completely understand what the company does—but I know they do it really well.

The teams were made up of an interesting mix of global young adults. As they went around the table introducing themselves, it went something like this:

"I'm twenty-six, was born in the Azores, and lived between there and Portugal as a child. Since then, I have worked in India and the U.K., and now I run the Sydney office."

It didn't seem like it was a good time to let them know I grew up in the same house in Whittier, California, that my mother just moved out of a few years ago. Yup, the world is flat.

Anyway, we spent two days with this dynamic group, and the one thing we never heard was fear. This fast-growing company (which is a bit of an understatement), with offices in six different countries and linking global communication, was made up of the most curious lot I've ever worked with—and I don't mean to imply that they were odd, but rather full of curiosity.

The questions they asked, both about organizational direction and personal leadership behaviors, were not tinged with protectiveness, hesitancy, or apprehension. With an abandon we rarely see, they threw themselves into the off-site work we gave them.

Midmorning of our second day, the company's CEO stood up and gave a quick update on an acquisition that had the potential to ignite an already catalytic company. He spoke for only seven or eight minutes, but I could see where the team got their confidence. Or at least why, as confident people, they were attracted to this organization and this leader.

In just a short time, he reminded the group of the courage that had gotten them to this point, the opportunity that this acquisition provided, and his confidence in this direction for the company. His demeanor and tone were kind and poised. He had an air of curiosity that demonstrated itself in the wonder he communicated about the future.

There it was again, that inverse relationship between curiosity and fear. This was a culture of curiosity. There was little fear.

Sometimes it *is* the leader who incites the fear. And not always in fire-breathing, angry, or obvious ways. We are currently working with a team that is at a critical juncture. If they cannot stand up to their leader, I am not convinced they will make it. They are afraid of him. At meetings they shut down, nod their heads even when they don't agree, and in general, have given up.

Their very strong sense is that the leader weighs every decision they make against what *he* would have decided. And to the degree that their decisions and opinions don't line up with his, he says they are wrong and that he can't trust them. The team members are tired and worn out.

The leader is charming and charismatic, and perhaps that is why it has taken them so long to figure out they're afraid of him. But the entire team is almost completely disengaged at this point, always trying to second-guess what the leader would choose rather than using that energy to research and debate fresh, new directions.

Fear deteriorates our high-level thinking capacities.

Fear, even just biologically, causes a fight-or-flight response from us. When we sense or anticipate the presence of danger, our adrenal glands and autonomic nervous systems respond in unconscious ways that propel us to either engage in a power struggle of attacking and blaming or to avoid and withdraw into resulting apathy.

Fear deteriorates our high-level thinking capacities lodged in our cerebral cortex (where logic and collaboration reside) and forces our reactions to emerge from our lower-level midbrain. Our cerebral cortex is our Ph.D. uncle, the one who is wise, reasonable, and dresses smartly. Our midbrain is our second cousin once removed who is missing two of his front teeth and drinks heavily.

Fear guarantees that second cousin Jethro will determine the culture of your organization.

Whatever you can do to recognize the level of fear that permeates your organization is a good thing. Moving from fear to curiosity has the potential to unlock all kinds of good things.

When people are released from anxiety and dread, they are freed up to create, innovate, and learn. Rather than being guarded, they openly consider what mistakes they may have made, how they can grow and be different, and what new ideas may emerge over time as their teams become fertile ground for new levels of creativity.

> **Moving from fear to curiosity has the potential to unlock all kinds of good things.**

Curiosity diminishes apprehension and trepidation. It fuels connections and understanding. It asks questions before it makes statements. It carries with it a sense of wonder and possibility and power that is deeply motivating and attractive. People like to be around genuinely curious people. There is a sense that although these people don't yet have the final answer, they would love it if you joined them in the journey of discovery. Who wouldn't want to work with someone like that?

Curiosity allows us to autopsy results that were less than we anticipated. Defensiveness and rationalization give way to learning and truth and growth. Risk taking is encouraged in curious climates, as is imagining and celebrating successes. Curiosity makes way for collaboration and anticipation of remarkable outcomes that we have only dreamed of before.

Perhaps the invitation to collaborate is one of the most powerful things that emerges from curiosity. Wondering what others would think, how they would solve this problem, what their contribution might be, and how that might add to a better outcome.

This is a very simple example. One of many. Early on at our time at Willow Creek, our senior pastor designed a ten-week series called "Yeah, God! Thanks for being _____." For ten weeks Bill wanted to unpack some of the key attributes of God in this creative format. But rather than sit in his office determining by himself what those ten attributes would be, he asked a bunch of us for ideas.

Instead of worrying he might not get the answers he wanted, he just invited people to respond to the title statement.

Curiosity diminishes apprehension and trepidation.

One of my suggestions—"Yeah, God! Thanks for being an equal opportunity employer"— was selected for the series. Each week, a banner was hung on the stage listing a different attribute of God. By the end of the series, ten different banners, all declaring the goodness of God, hung from the auditorium ceiling.

Here's why this is a very simple example. This was not

a huge deal. No one knew that was my contribution. I wasn't asked to preach that sermon. As I recall, they asked some guy named John Ortberg to do that. I didn't tell anyone it had been my idea.

But I'll tell you what did happen. Every week after that sermon, when I looked up and saw that banner hanging there, I welled up a bit inside. I was so proud and happy that I was able to contribute. I got to help. I got to be a part of creating and designing something that had an impact on people and showed them God more clearly. I know, it was just a title.

But it was also a message. This was a place, an organization, a community, where the curiosity of the leader and of the culture would make room for me. I could play here. I didn't need or want to be the only one doing it, I just wanted to be an active part. Curiosity is pretty powerful stuff. Perhaps not for cats, but definitely for mongooses.

As we talked about in the last chapter, Scot McKnight writes that people basically are open to change in two circumstances: on a quest or in a crisis. When self-motivated people go on a quest, they are open to new information. The journey presumes adventure and learning. In leadership development, we are looking for people like this. As leaders, we want to be people on a quest. The journey invokes a kind of inquisitiveness that causes a person to be full of questions and thoughtfulness.

A crisis is a bit of a different animal. How we respond in one is a sort of barometer of our internal cores. In addition to that, if we respond to crisis with curiosity, we begin to ask the important questions: Where is God in this? What will God do? What will I learn about God that I do not already know?

These are questions that deepen our faith and shape our leadership. Of course, some crises are so intense that our only response is a dark night of the soul that reflects our despair. And sometimes our best response is that quiet humility that asks no questions, the painful crying out to God, and stillness.

But there are other times, when the crisis is just under the threshold of hopelessness, that the curiosity factor can kick in and transform our responses. Over time, a leader who responds to crises with curiosity will begin to infuse a confidence in the organization. Obstacles are not as formidable when one is calmly asking questions and considering what an appropriate response ought to be. This confidence is necessary and contagious.

This is another thing that Max DePree has taught me. (If you are not already sick of that phrase, you will be by the end of this book. Actually, come to think of it, I should probably give Max a percentage of every book sold. Note to self: As soon as my last kid graduates from college, I will do that.)

Max taught me that asking questions is one of the most important tasks of a leader, but more importantly, a good leader must start by figuring out the right questions. It's not good enough just to ask questions. The *right* questions are necessary in order to guarantee the right answers. So it becomes the necessary work of a leader to spend time thinking: Are we asking the right questions?

Recently one of my partners and I were working with a potential client. Their team was encountering problems in the areas of decision making and accountability. They wanted to schedule a one-day session focusing on goal setting, and they sent us some team testing they had done the year prior.

We talked with the team leaders for a while, listening to their stories and asking some salient questions. Then we told them that just setting goals was not their main problem.

"I don't think that whether you make this event a one-day or a two-day experience is the most important question," said my partner, David. "I think the most important question here is 'What will you do with whatever results and information we give you?'"

Clearly after they had done the team assessments a year prior, those beautifully colored and charted pages had found their way into a notebook and had sat there for the year. They already had information that had the potential to transform their team, and they had done nothing with it. Now they were calling us, a different consulting firm, to ask for help.

And even more than just getting paid, we want to work with motivated teams that are bent on transformation. Just a little shift in the question turns the thinking around 180 degrees.

what's Barcelona
Got to Do with It?

FOR MANY YEARS, BARCELONA was rarely a first-stop tourist destination. Instead, it was the kind of place that usually got added onto the end of a trip when travelers had a few extra days to spare or needed a place to spend the night before catching a plane.

But recently, Barcelona's reputation has been changing. In 2000, approximately twenty million travelers crisscrossed the Barcelona airport. A mere six years later that number grew to thirty million. Today, Barcelona is the number-two tourist destination in Europe.

So what happened?

The 1992 Summer Olympics. I find it very interesting

that something that happened in 1992 could have such stunning repercussions fourteen years later.[1] Let's start there.

Leaders, we are an impatient lot. Faster is better, quick is good, speed is our constant companion. Isn't it funny how something so necessary can also be so detrimental? And here we are, back to managing tensions. Leaders need impatience. Living with a sense of urgency is part of our wiring; it's also a very appropriate response to both creating momentum and reacting to a hurt and damaged world.

However, impatience and urgency can wound people, elicit second-rate decisions, and cause us to cut corners in ways that substitute short-term wins for long-term change. The best way to overcome these issues is not to slow down to a turtle's pace, but rather to add to our leader's repertoire the beauty and strength of perseverance, patience, and endurance. And to know what to use when.

Everyone I worked with in the emergency room understood this choreographed dance of urgency and patience. In that department, there was this almost explosive sense of speed, alongside methodical, ordered precision that, when fused together, yielded life. That is the dance of the leader.

---

[1] Information about Barcelona in this chapter is taken from Christine Spolar, "Barcelona Shows What Olympics Can Mean," *Chicago Tribune*, August 12, 2007.

Okay, back to Barcelona.

Getting the city ready to host the Summer Games was all about the Olympics. But it ended up becoming the springboard for the city's future. I don't think anyone on the planning committee was thinking, *And while we're at it, let's leverage this preparation to create a Barcelona that will move into the future as one of the top cities in Europe!*

But often, that's what happens when you revitalize something. It has ripple effects far beyond what you were expecting. In Bible times, especially in the Old Testament, the reinvigorating of a city was cause for celebration in the people and in the country. It was a sign of the life of God breathed fresh.

For Barcelona, the work of rebirth paid off. Not only were the 1992 Olympics judged by many to be among the best of the modern games, but the subsequent propulsion of Barcelona into the category of top cities was a lasting result of that city's efforts.

Preparing the city required a Herculean overhaul, not just a fresh coat of paint and a new stadium. And for a long time the people of Barcelona endured the chaos, inconvenience, and noise that they hoped would ready their beloved home for the eyes of the world.

With the clock ticking, they tore out old warehouses and reclaimed industrial wastelands that had once been oceanfront properties. Engineers and architects and construction workers labored, building an infrastructure of highways, access routes, pools, and tracks. State-of-the-art stadiums were constructed, bus routes were added, gardens were planted.

Urban planning was integrated with Olympic preparation, and the result was that Barcelona, a city of living neighborhoods, put its best face on for the world to see. A city was overhauled from the inside out, and the best of Barcelona, its boroughs and fifty thousand volunteer "ambassadors for the city" were amassed to add hospitality to what the visitors would experience when they came for the games.

Before the Olympic torch was even lit, the city's historic Gothic churches, lively tapas bars, and art collections were spotlighted. While the 1992 games lured guests into this transformed city, the revitalization kept them coming for years to follow.

Sometimes a major overhaul is exactly what is needed. I can't tell you when that is true. Believe me, if there were a formula for this stuff, I would either be following it myself or writing a book about it and living in Tahiti.

More than orchestrating major overhauls, however, good leaders must always try to keep the big picture at the forefront of their minds, all the while directing and integrating the individual components with the whole. Components that when left to stand alone would be no more than small movements, but that together create seismic shifts.

Prior to 1992, somebody in Barcelona was sitting in meetings saying, "Okay, let's talk about the engineering issues and figure out how each of these transportation changes will support the whole—where the stadiums are being built and where the hotels are.

"What are our costs and time schedules, and are they reasonably aggressive? Will these changes support the capacity we are anticipating?

"Now, what about the gardens, the landscaping, the restaurants, and the footpaths?

"Are we revitalizing our city without losing its heart and soul?" These people were discussing, deciding, and implementing the parts while weaving them into the whole. They were doing the looking behind and looking ahead that all great leaders must do. Honoring the past, holding on to the values that created the best of it, and all the while carving out a future that is better.

Sometimes a major overhaul is needed.

It's easy to read about Barcelona's success and overlook the painful chaos and unclear outcomes that accompany such major overhauls. To be naive about what it feels like in the middle.

But the middle is where leading gets hard. It's when you're so far into it that you can't remember what it was that first convinced you this was all necessary, but you are too far from the end to see the light.

But when the end result is Barcelona, it provides a beautiful and inspirational rearview-mirror glance that reminds us just how worth it it was to keep going.

I was at a church recently that had just emerged from that tunnel. This church had a history of resistance to change. I know that's hard to imagine, but stick with me. They had many people on staff who shouldn't have been, a long history of never talking about giving, and a comfort level with the way things were that was impressive.

Sometimes a major overhaul is needed.

The congregation was doing nothing but growing older, both in age and viewpoints. The average attendee was old. The facilities were old. The style of worship was old. Then, through a convergence of conditions seemingly orchestrated by the Holy Spirit, things began to change. And it wasn't the kind of incremental, safe change that replaces the bulletin's white paper with beige or buys new crayons for the children's room. No, not that kind. We're talking Barcelona.

Not everyone liked it, but over the course of about six

months, six or seven key leaders were appropriately invited to either get on board with the new direction or find another place to serve. New staff members with fresh eyes and fresh spirits were brought on, changing the texture of the leadership community. The pastor began talking about giving, and this church embarked on its first capital giving campaign in over thirty years.

Multisite video venues were started within a twenty-mile radius of the main church campus, along with two church plants in nearby communities. The scale of change was enormous.

The change was conducted in a highly collaborative but directive way. Input was encouraged at many points, but at the same time the leadership team refused to abdicate its responsibility for leading. The congregation was well informed and included when appropriate, but there was never any doubt that this change was to be permanent. This church was never going back to the way it was before.

Any other questions?

And it was all embedded in the gospel. Every bit of it. Jesus at the center and an authentic relationship with a good and great God led to transformational discipleship and vibrant evangelism. The desire to provide a positive atmosphere for their children and visitors led to refurbishing the children's rooms. The desire to touch lives in a new way created multiple sites and church plants throughout the community.

The budgets were a stretch, but not unnecessarily extravagant. An ambitious budget was added for missions, both locally and internationally. Sweeping revisions, startling change.

I recently attended their weekend services, and they were celebrating some of these things. The capital campaign had just tallied up the "beyond tithes" commitments, and found that they were 30 percent over their target. The room erupted with applause when this was announced at each service.

That same weekend, they showed a video from their first church plant, which was launching that day approximately twenty miles away. People cheered and clapped as they watched those folks set up and get ready for their first weekend service. And then the pastor gave one of the most powerful sermons on God I've heard in a long time.

Fresh winds.

A new day, new ways of doing the ancient church.

Yet still clinging to the values and cementing the core. God's Spirit is always making room for more at the table.

Barcelona in our backyards.

In addition to all the glorious things we talked about at the beginning of this chapter, great leadership enabled

Barcelona to pay off the construction costs two years early with the steady stream of sports revenue that came out of Olympic and the post-Olympic stadium use.

Two years early. No one had predicted that. It was simply an unexpected outcome of a job well done. But there's also another side to the Barcelona story. In the midst of all the amazing things, both during the Olympics and now in the ensuing tourism the city enjoys, a few things got lost. While Barcelona was shining, six hundred and twenty-four people were displaced from their homes. With the sweeping changes, the neglected waterfront and its affordable, albeit decrepit, housing was swept away. People lost their homes.

It may be tempting at this point to overlook that fact by comparing it to the glittering results and running the numbers: six hundred twenty-four people versus millions. But that's too easy.

In addition to those initially displaced, hundreds more poor and elderly residents have since been forced out due to increasing housing prices. Beyond housing, the airport, once sufficient for the needs of Barcelona, quickly surpassed its capacity and now shows significant signs of strain and cracks.

So all the good stuff . . . well, it's only part of the story. The planners missed some things. They overlooked several important issues. In the midst of a complete overhaul, some things slipped through the cracks. Barcelona isn't a complete success story. It's a whole story. It's a place where some truly remarkable things happened and are happening. And it's a place where some not-so-good things happened and are happening.

But here's the deal. If they could transform the city to the degree they did, then we know they have the ability and power to fix the low-income housing and the airport as well. Absolutely. The same ingenuity, forethought, and planning that made Barcelona the number-two travel destination can certainly get its arms around these issues and tackle them. Probably in a very impressive way.

Leadership is about living in that tension between the beautiful, successful, transformed Barcelona *and* the displaced, overlooked, poor Barcelona. It is not one story or the other; it is both. Good leadership changes things. Relentlessly. Significantly. And after it celebrates the movement, it takes another look to see what might have been overlooked. Then good leadership goes at it again.

I just got back from speaking at a church leadership conference in Germany, a country where 4 percent of the population attends church. After the conference, I preached on Sunday in a church of nearly three hundred people, a megachurch by Germany's standards. Just a few years ago, they had averaged around seventy people. I was curious as to what had transpired between then and now.

Apparently, they had begun to outgrow the building they were meeting in, so they started looking around and found a great deal on an abandoned American tank warehouse from World War II.

Great irony there. They were able to purchase the larger space, and began gutting the building. All of a sudden, the

Good leadership changes things. Relentlessly. Significantly.

new activity and the possibilities for the future began to inspire people. People in the church stepped forward and began to design the interior of the building, teach classes, and lead home groups. They used this new era to invite their neighbors and friends, and amazingly, people who up to this point had been uninterested agreed to come to church. They, too, had been watching the transformations and they were intrigued.

Something in all of that change had captured people's attention. That is what the gospel does: It captures people's attention. That's what was going on in Acts 2 as well. People watched and were attracted—the gospel as a magnet.

Now, let me be clear about what I am *not* saying. The gospel is not about a building program. In fact, there are many churches that shouldn't do a building program. A lot of times, far too much of church budgets are being spent on buildings.

Buildings are important, but they are not the gospel. My point is not about structures but about change. Sometimes we need to shake things up, to make large-scale changes that get people's attention.

In 1 Thessalonians, Paul says that the gospel came to the people not just in word, but also in power. I want our churches to be places where the power of the gospel is seen and felt both organizationally and individually.

When John and I moved into the area where we are currently living, scores of people told us about one particular neighborhood restaurant. The reports were glowing, and the name popped up so often that we knew we wanted to try it. Each time we drove by it, we talked about going in. When we finally stopped and had dinner there, it was a wonderful experience. And then, we became part of that group of people who were always encouraging others to go there.

Interesting progression that ought to cause us to think.

ch . . . ch . . . ch . . . *Changes*

RECENTLY I HEARD SOMEONE say that when the change on the outside of your organization is greater than the change on the inside of it, you are in trouble.

Uh-oh.

If you are a leader, you know that change is a constant, and leading through and to change may be one of the most important and difficult things you do. The problem is that for most people, change ranks right up there next to public speaking and having your toenails removed with pliers. Not everyone, mind you, but most.

So one of the most precarious and delicate dances leaders must do is to discern which areas within their organizations are most in need of change—and how much—while at the same time balancing the capacity within the organizations to assimilate and gravitate toward that change. We have all seen leaders who did too much changing too quickly, blowing up their organizations with their lack of finesse and inability to pace well. We have also seen leaders who never did more than make slight variations on what already existed, and then stood by helplessly as the organization lost its effectiveness and imploded.

Trying to avoid both of those scenarios will drive you crazy. If an equation existed that would direct you to that elusive middle ground, someone would have published it. It doesn't exist. Leadership is an art (Max DePree said and wrote that).

Change builds on the past. It asks the question "What has led us up to today?" and finds authentic ways to honor what is behind us. It understands and does not underestimate the role of the past in shaping the future. With clear eyes, change discerns the problems and dysfunctions of the past, but with those same eyes it also sees with great appreciation the best of the past—those things that have provided the very foundation on which you currently stand.

Leadership is an art.
—Max DePree

The past holds obstacles, often through a romanticized view of "the way it was" or in the words "we've never done it that way before." But the past also holds promise. Looking back, we can see with clarity the values that must not change even when the practices do. In the past, we find roots for our changing methods and expressions. We discover opportunities to express our admiration for those who lived the past and reassure them that we are building on the best of it, not ignoring or neglecting it.

Change lives in the reality of the present. As we saw in the "Stone Ships" chapter, the first job of a leader is to define the current reality. Sounds simple enough, but actually it takes a great deal of courage to do. Almost no one wants to hear your definition of reality. Living in the past or in a comfortably distorted view of the present is oddly preferable. The reality of the present includes the truth about where we currently are and whether or not we currently have the right team to move us into the future. What are our strengths and weaknesses? Where are we failing? Where are we succeeding? How do we define both of these things so that they mean something?

Defining present reality requires painful diagnostics that show us where to direct our energy and attention. Defining present reality is the "you are here" point on the map. Every journey into the future needs a starting place.

Defining present reality is a collaborative conversation that results in getting everyone pointed in the same direction.

Change sketches out the future. At first, it's just a vague outline, but with enough definition that our hearts beat a little faster and we wonder together if it just might be possible. Over time, the outline becomes clearer and begins to shape the horizons, as we imagine what might be and see progress toward that distant shape. The opportunities and possibilities are so breathtaking that they scare us a bit, but they also compel us. The future is only motivating when it promises more and better and different and relevant and new and fresh. Change brings those gifts.

The chance to transform individuals and institutions, as well as situations and conditions, is what makes the future so bright. Without those things, the future is merely a repetition of the past, just in front of us rather than behind.

Change can be difficult because there is no guaranteed road map. There is no Auto Club of Change that you can go to and get a clearly marked route.

Almost everyone I know has photos in frames on display throughout the house. Striking pictures of families growing through the years, from just-born babies to pubescent teenagers to young adults with families of their own. Most have pictures of vacations that hold indelible memories and photos of grandparents who are no longer with us.

But no one I know has a framed photo of the future. We don't see that as clearly. It is not as indelible in our minds as the past or the present. It is unclear and vague. That is one of the reasons leading change is so difficult. But here's what I know: We will move forward when our hope for the future is greater than our stories of the past.

We have no idea of the stories of change and redeemed lives that await us. We have yet to see the difference we can make in this beautiful and broken world. But vision is about imagining the pictures that will be displayed in those photo frames five years from now and twenty years from now. And liking what we see enough to work hard toward it.

We will move forward when our hope for the future is greater than our stories of the past.

A wise leader expects to face resistance to change, as well as a dizzying array of other responses. A few years back, when our kids were nine, seven, and five, we needed to tell them that we were moving from our home in Southern California to the beautiful tundra that is called Chicago. As a second-generation Californian, I had not yet warmed to this idea by the time we needed to tell the children. But tell them we did.

Because it was a particularly busy time at church and John had a lot to do in preparation for the move, his idea was for me to tell them. Since his idea was *not* going to happen, I had another (better) one. The kids and I would meet him at a McDonald's near his office for dinner. Fortunately our kids were at an age when a Happy Meal could cure almost anything. Or so we thought.

We got everyone settled around the table with their steaming food in front of them, and then Mommy and Daddy told a nice story about a family who loved each other very much and was going to move to a faraway land.

Once Johnny, our five-year-old, heard that Chicago was the land where the Bulls and Michael Jordan lived, and that the house would most likely have a basement, and that there would be snow, he was in. Our oldest daughter, Laura, however, didn't even wait to hear how the story ended before bolting from the table, running to the parking lot, and locking herself in the car.

Mallory, torn between the two reactions, landed somewhere in between. But once we got to Chicago, she began to show significant signs of sadness and fear that revealed her true feelings about the move.

Now, almost fifteen years later, we've been back in California for five years (*Thank You, God!*). And all of our kids would tell you they are glad that we lived in Chicago.

After that first, somewhat difficult year of adjustment, they made lifelong friends and memories there. But their initial response was mostly negative, and it took time for them to be fully grateful for it.

When things change, you can and must expect resistance, questions, and hesitance. Change is not a passive process. Leaders must lead, and they must expect people to go through several phases as they go into the change. The more collaboration there is between the leadership and others in the organization, the more smoothly the process will typically go. The success of this change process depends on authentic collaboration.

Initially almost everyone, at every level, will have some kind of **reaction**. That seems so obvious that it's almost unnecessary to say, but maybe not. You must look for the signs of those reactions and use those as your cues as to how to best assist people as they move through the change process. Some will react with questions that you need to answer. Others will become cynical, and you will need to address that. Start by naming the reaction and then plumbing for the fear that most likely underlies it.

There are too many possible reactions to list them all, or even a portion. Just remember, as much as you may think this isn't true, you do not want submission without reservation. No, really, you don't. It is okay and necessary for people to have their questions and their mistrust. They need time and explanation; they need to understand and be able to speak into it and be a part of shaping and being heard.

While people are reacting, you and the leadership team need to be finding ways to assist them in their reactions. You will have to give massive amounts of time with people during high change seasons. Spend the majority of that time *before* the change is implemented, not after. If you wait until after, you will have much more work to do, and you will have dishonored people in the process.

After a period of reaction, most people and organizations will move into a period of **adjustment**. This phase tends to be quieter than *reaction*, but don't be fooled. Many things are happening during the adjustment period. If you have helped well during the first phase, this next phase is largely about an internal "buy-in" that allows people to integrate the new with the old and mourn the past while growing increasingly excited about the future.

If you rush the first phase, this second phase will still be a quiet one, but what will be growing in that silence will be resistance, anger, and combat. Whatever is happening, the end of this phase is often marked by movement. This movement is either in the form of folks getting on board, directly fighting with you, and/or leaving.

Those who stay will mark the third phase of **initiative**. The main question people will have at this point is "What will my part be?" During this period, people begin to align or realign their giftedness and their energies to the new vision; together they begin pointing themselves in the same direction. The job of a leader now is to connect and engage as many people as possible. This phase is the payoff of having been diligent in phase one and patient in phase two. And it is a wonder to behold, an organization doing a 180-degree turn, even if it means losing a few people in the process. It can be one of the deeply satisfying payoffs of great leadership.

All of this time, the leadership team supports, coaches, and encourages each other as everyone on the team permeates the organization and does the work of change. They debrief together, "autopsy" results, learn, grow, and challenge one another. They do midcourse corrections and celebrate.

Resistance isn't the only thing to expect when you're implementing change. To seriously consider making changes means to seriously consider making mistakes.

There are few things I enjoy more than a rousing speech on the importance of mistakes. In order to create an environment of both innovation and personal growth, it is necessary that we make allowances, and even applaud mistakes.

I find it inspiring when leaders who are very successful have a long list of mistakes that they credit for launching them toward all the achievements they now enjoy.

So why do mistakes feel so hard? Why is my response to them not celebration, but embarrassment and disappointment? Why do I feel that when I make those mistakes, others aren't celebrating either but are sharing in my disappointment? Why do I want to hide rather than be open about the mistakes? Everyone loves a winner. I wonder what the yang of that statement is—I think I know.

When our oldest daughter went off to college, before I left her dorm room, I handed her a small package. She opened it to find a hand-sized journal. I told her it was a "mistake journal." Because she is a firstborn child, I thought she needed some practice in getting comfortable with mistakes.

I told her that every night just before she went to bed, she should open it up and write down three mistakes she made that day. And if she was going to put them in writing, they ought to be good ones, not made-up ones. Then, she should put that little journal under her pillow, and fall asleep realizing that (1) the world was still spinning on its axis, (2) tomorrow was another day, and (3) God still loved her.

I think leaders need mistake journals. Unless we get

comfortable both in our mistakes and what we learn from them, we inadvertently create organizational cultures of fear and sameness. Change and innovation are natural outcomes of a relaxed reaction to mistakes. On a personal level, the Christlike transformation that we all talk about actually begins to happen. Our mistakes are a remarkable catalyst for growth.

When a culture is created where fear of failure is decreased, people are better able to quickly move beyond the understandable first reactions of embarrassment and disappointment, and lower their defenses enough so that new learning begins to occur. People rarely do their best or most creative work in an environment of fear. Much like the fight-or-flight response, fear limits our options.

So a couple of steps in becoming a leader who shapes people and organizations through their mistakes:

Start by admitting your own. Get comfortable enough in your own skin and in the forgiveness of God to start telling stories on yourself. Admit past failures and what got you there. Connect your immature behavior to the mistake. My own need to be important and my lack of verbal discipline are just two things that have gotten me in trouble with the leaders of one ministry, and into deep interpersonal conflict with others.

Fear limits our options.

And don't just keep your stories in the past. It's much easier to talk about mistakes when the relationships have been patched up and you've already tied a neat bow on the incident. It's another level of vulnerability to talk, appropriately, about current and ongoing struggles.

Autopsy the mistakes. Few leadership teams take the time or have the courage to lay a mistake on the table, take it apart, and try to understand how it happened. The most likely result is that people will have to take differing levels of responsibility for what happened, and that takes a kind of humility and openness that is rare. But without it, transformation doesn't have a chance.

> **Our ability to love is reflected in our capacity to forgive.**

Our ability to love is reflected in our capacity to forgive, and mistakes give us a public opportunity for both. Autopsies that lead to forgiveness and learning rather than grudge holding and blaming create organizations that are moving into the future well with God, not paralyzed by fear and relational wholeness. God's fresh winds of the Spirit are always blowing.

Perhaps our mistakes give us fresh eyes to catch that wind.

when to *Worry*

RECENTLY A GUY CALLED our office. He was the CEO of a midsize company that had enjoyed early and explosive growth, but now he found his team in a season of stagnation. He spent a fair amount of time explaining to me the specifics of their history as a business and answering some of the questions I was asking to better understand his challenges.

Then he said, "Here's the bottom line. We all like each other, we get along great, and we never disagree. We just aren't moving forward."

I offered that those things were inexorably linked.

Most teams view conflict as a sign of serious problems.

It's easy to mistake displays of quick agreement, early consensus, and lack of objections for signs of health. But teams that get along all of the time and never disagree ought to make you nervous. Really nervous. Palm-sweating, palpitation-inducing nervous.

It's funny how looking good on the outside often betrays some serious stuff going on inside. Like the runner who drops dead of a heart attack. It's a surprise, but he's still dead.

Here's the truth: Conflict is basically energy, and, harkening back to Physics 101, you know that energy has to go somewhere. The good news is that as the leader, you can decide where that energy goes:

Underground, in the roll of the eyes, the silent response, the meeting after the meeting where people declare laughingly, "That'll never work!"

Or . . .

In the meeting, face-to-face, no holding back, robust debate of the issues, no grudges afterward.

I would pick number two every time. The problem is, and we all know it, that it's not as simple as just picking a number. Too often, all the things listed in number one are hidden behind the mask of an approving nod: *Sure, that sounds like a great idea. Yes I am behind this 100 percent.* Malicious compliance. Something deep down in your gut is reminding you that approving nods rarely result in follow-through. When that happens, it's a sure sign that conflict has gone underground.

Getting along, just not moving forward.

Let me tell you how I know so much about this. I have some pretty impressive credentials when it comes to conflict. Actually, I have often been the one doing the subversive conflict thing. I definitely did the roll of the eyes—only in my mind's eye—during the meeting. And then once we got behind closed doors, I could openly roll my eyes with the best of them, garnishing great laughter as I delicately mocked the decision. It was delicious, the admiration I gained. I had quite a following, all of us cowards.

Funny how something that was once so much fun is now the source of great embarrassment to me. But I'll have to say this about really embarrassing situations: Eventually you either leave or learn. I'm happy to say that most often—not always, but most often—I learned.

And as I was learning, I also ended up leading people who were just like I had been. Leadership irony, I suppose. Annoying for sure. But at least I could offer a little grace with my irritation.

So, back to worrying about when there isn't conflict.

Great teams *need* spirited, unfiltered debate. They need it to clear the air, they need it to trust each other, and they need it to make important decisions worth committing to. Great teams need leaders who are comfortable with debate and actually require it.

One of my colleagues, Kent Bechler, often says that the further up you go in an organization, the less truth you will hear. For that reason, wise leaders surround themselves with people who aren't afraid to tell the truth.

I was sitting in my office one day when Steve, my associate director, stuck his head in the door and said, "Do you have a minute?"

Now leadership is a relationally intensive endeavor and leaders must provide those they lead with access. But you already know that this is a chapter on conflict, so we'll cover that issue of access and relationship in another chapter.

Sure Steve, come on in! Glad to have you in my office. Glad you are benefiting from my often-open-door policy. Love working with you. What's on your mind, my friend?

"Well, I want to talk to you about something, and I'm not the only one who feels this way."

Not a great way to start, but I was the one who had invited him in.

Please, tell me more.

Steve explained that when I first arrived to lead Axis, the one thing he liked (this kid was not earning any brownie points) was my meetings. He said that it had been a long time since someone had put as much time and thought and preparation into the Axis meetings.

And then he made an abrupt shift and said something like, "I don't know what has been occupying your time now, but your meetings suck."

Okay . . .

So, Steve, how long did you say you had been looking for another place to work?

Who does this guy think he is? What is he, twenty-four? Is he kidding me? Does he have any idea what my days are like? how much work I do? how often I protect Axis and the staff from all the other organizational issues I am working on?

It's amazing how many thoughts can flash through your mind in a millisecond, while there is still a pleasant smile plastered on your face. It's also amazing how sometimes, amid all those thoughts, a rational one rises like a phoenix. I asked myself, *What part of what he is saying is not true?* Notice, that's a different question than *What part of what he is saying do I not like?*

The truth was, Steve was right. When I first started leading Axis, I was so excited. So grateful for such a wonderful opportunity, so thankful to be allowed to lead in an area for which I had so much passion. And I threw the best of who I was into it.

I thought about meetings all the time. Patrick Lencioni talks a lot about meetings as the places where most of leadership happens. A leader who says he doesn't like meetings is a lot like a surgeon saying, "Yeah, if it wasn't for operating, I'd really like my job." If you are a leader, meetings *are* your job. And I took that seriously. At least at first.

Pat also says that your people should look forward to meetings more than they would the invitation to a movie. Yeah, how's that for clarifying the gap?

So when I first started leading Axis, I thought about the purpose of each meeting. I asked myself who needed to be there, what information I needed to gather beforehand, and what I could do to make the meetings more creative, fast paced, and fun. I also always tried to end on time and leave people wanting more.

But then, life got busy. Actually leadership got busy. I had other plates to spin, other things to think about and give my energy to, and before I knew it, even I didn't want to go to my meetings.

I guess I figured that since I got my meetings off to a good start (and that is probably a great way to begin a new leadership run, with a shift in the tone of the meetings that in itself declares, "This is a new day"), I could check that off my list. No one told me that in order to keep our meetings energized, I needed to continue spending time on them. I guess no one should have had to tell me that.

So I was left with this: What part of what Steve said to me wasn't true?

And then, in that split second, another thought showed up: *What kind of courage had it taken Steve to initiate this conversation with me?*

With the help of those two thoughts, I asked Steve to tell me more, and we had a great conversation about how to rectify the situation. Steve, God bless him, had given me a gift. A gift wrapped in a package that almost caused me to miss it, but a gift nonetheless.

Steve had given me the gift of conflict. The gift that keeps giving, even when you don't want it.

Really, no thank you. I can't accept it. Really, you shouldn't have. Really.

But here's the funny thing about conflict. Conflict is a spiritual formation practice. You don't read much about it, what with all the attention on quiet times

Conflict is a spiritual formation practice.

and journaling and listening to praise songs. Maybe that's too bad, and maybe we are the poorer because of it.

Conflict is this crucible for change. It is the environment

in which we can take some of our best and deepest looks at ourselves and our organizations. It is the tension that stirs us to resolution, the conversation that leads to understanding and apology. Conflict prompts an internal look, a conversation with God, a repentance that is rare.

I remember a time that I was angry with another leader I worked with at Willow Creek. And one of the things I loved the most about the culture at Willow was the commitment to conflict resolution and change. So I went to my boss and explained the whole situation from my perspective, which of course I was sure was the only one. Wisely, my boss set up a meeting with me and the other leader. I had *so* been hoping that

Conflict is this crucible for change.

wouldn't be the outcome. Surely, I thought, my boss could just go to this other leader and whack him up the side of the head, and we could be done with it. But *no,* we had to actually *do* the Matthew 18 thing. I was pretty sure that Matthew 18 was just a suggestion Jesus had made as a last-ditch effort when gossip and resentment just weren't working anymore.

So there we sat, the bad-mean leader, my boss, and me. We talked and listened, explained and shared frustrations. Then at one point, my boss asked me what I thought this other leader's motives were.

Oh, yeah right . . . I am *so* not going there. I will just present the facts, Your Honor. No speculation here.

My boss went on to explain that we weren't just here to talk about behaviors but also about motivations. Because one determines the other, and you can't change one without understanding the other.

So down we went, where the air was damp and heavy, the visibility not very good, and the oxygen saturation low. It was slow-moving, difficult, and dangerous work. It was a long meeting, and we were exhausted. But here's what emerged:

The bad-mean leader was operating out of power and image management. I was being a martyr, avoider, and gossiper. We sat for a long time talking about the truth of those things and working toward admitting and resolving them, to the extent you can do that in one conversation. We talked about what it meant—what it really meant—to live and lead out of community and to be followers of Christ, and how that affected the motives we had uncovered.

Things aren't always fifty-fifty. In fact, I'd say they rarely are. And this was no exception. Bad-mean leader bore a bit more weight of responsibility. But the amazing thing was that bad-mean leader was the one to bring that up. (Believe me, this book is full of times when I was the one bearing the higher percentage. And if you are tempted to think it is petty and unnecessary to determine percentages, I pretty strongly disagree with that. It may be difficult to determine, but I think it is important.)

That conversation, laden with conflict, was the catalyst for deep growth. We did some hard repair work, both separately and in the context of our relationship, and today, bad-mean leader and I are still good friends.

With such a good outcome, it's a wonder we don't go looking for conflict.

As you've no doubt figured out by now, one of the mentors I have been blessed with is Max DePree. For many years, Max was the CEO of Herman Miller, which was voted one of the top fifty companies in the country at which to work. Max has taught me *so* many things about leadership, and this was one of the first.

Max described a time when he and a handful of other CEOs had gathered for a meeting. During one of the breaks, the talk turned to what CEOs should do when they receive an anonymous e-mail or letter that is critical of their leadership. To a person, the response around the table was a proud and dismissive "throw it away."

I'll never forget Max's silence. Sort of the preview to an alternative perspective. He listened for a while and then spoke. "I read every one of them. I consider if there might be some truth in them. I think the fact that the complaints are anonymous, while not the best method of communication, is a completely different issue than whether or not part or all of what they are saying is legitimate."

That got everyone's attention. What kind of humility and courage was at the core of a man who could graciously and authentically respond that way? The admiration around the circle was evident.

Even anonymous conflict is worth considering as a possible catalyst for growth and change. I figure if God can speak to Balaam through the mouth of an ass, he can speak to me through anyone.

I vividly remember an Axis meeting that was filled with very uncomfortable conflict. We had been working on our spring retreat for about six months. In addition to our weekend services, our home groups, and our serving opportunities, our spring retreat was one of the most strategic events we had.

Nearly half of the Axis community would attend these three days in Wisconsin (hey, in the Midwest your choices are limited)—a great combination of leadership, core attendees, and people new to the Axis community. We worked hard to build deeply into all three groups.

Typically the leaders arrived on Friday evening to participate in activities planned just for them. We provided a great meal with a lot of storytelling and vision. We provided training on specific leadership skills and communicated what each person's role would be for the next two days, toward both our regular and new retreat attendees.

Saturday and Sunday would then be filled with icebreakers, teaching, singing, small-group time, videos, and highlights of the best of Axis. Every year, this retreat was one of the most important and defining things we did.

So on the Tuesday before the retreat, our Axis team met to go over final details of the retreat. I started the meeting by talking through the first three or four things our leaders would experience when they arrived, and the importance of each one of them. Then, using those as the framework for our discussion, I turned to our director of operations and said, "Fred (you know that's not his name), how are the final plans for those first few elements?"

This was not a trick question. We had been working on this three-day event for six months. Fred and I, both in team meetings and in one-on-ones, had had these discussions. This was just supposed to be the final run-through before the retreat.

But Fred said, "Uh, you know what? Those things aren't in place yet."

Knowing I had misunderstood what I thought I'd

heard—I *thought* I had heard him say, "Those things aren't in place yet"—I asked him to repeat himself.

Sure enough, I had heard him correctly the first time. Did I mention that the retreat was three days away *and* that we had been working on it for six months? Or at least I thought so.

In a rare moment of maturity, I knew that if I allowed myself to go with my immediate reaction, well, you know. So I looked around to see if I was going to get any help from anyone else on the team. Didn't look like it. They were all looking at the ground and shifting nervously. Up to this point, I was still the main person holding people accountable, which really means we were not yet functioning as a cohesive team. We had not yet arrived at that peer-to-peer accountability that defines a team.

So I took a deep breath and asked Fred to leave the meeting for twenty minutes. I looked at my watch and gave him a time to return. He slowly got up and walked away. I looked at my team, waiting for someone, anyone, to make eye contact with me. When a couple of them did, I asked, "So how do you guys feel about what just happened?"

At this point I know a lot of people who would say I shouldn't have sent Fred away. I shouldn't have asked the team to talk about it. I should have taken care of it just between Fred and me. But I also know that a lot of people would completely agree that what I was doing was holding someone accountable for doing the job he was being paid—with tithe dollars—to do.

It's a mistake to take care of conflicts in a one-on-one when the infraction is at the level of team, a mistake that keeps teams dysfunctional. Over the previous six months, Fred had repeatedly assured us that these things were being taken care of, so there was the issue of truth to deal with as well. So many issues in that one response.

But when I asked the team how they felt about what had just happened, the only response I got was a quiet muttering of understanding. A mumbling acknowledgment that the situation was unfortunate, but not much beyond that. So I put it another way.

"How many of you got everything done for the retreat that was your responsibility?"

Every hand went up. I knew they would.

"How many of you were thinking that between now and the retreat on Friday, you could work your usual schedule, going home on time?"

They could see where this was going. When it dawned on them that Fred's malpractice was going to cost them, the conversation began in earnest. Some expressed their frustration, as well as anger that they had been lied to for months.

When twenty minutes had passed, Fred returned to a different team. One by one, we went around the circle and addressed Fred, looking him in the eye as we spoke. Each team member registered the frustration and anger we were all experiencing. It was awkward and uncomfortable, for sure. It would have been so nice if we could have avoided it, but the cost would have been too great.

But here's what really made me proud and hopeful: To a person, each team member finished his or her complaint by taking a slice of Fred's work and promising to work with him to make sure it got done by Friday. They expressed their dissatisfaction, but they also covered his back; they pitched in, in spite of the way he had shirked his duties, and they made sure the work got done.

By the end of the meeting, we had moved from being concerned only about our own areas of responsibility to living in the big picture together. We moved from wanting to avoid difficult issues to really dealing with them. And though we probably emerged a bit bruised, it was nothing that couldn't be healed. And actually, in the end, our team was healed in a way that made it stronger than it was before.

Not long ago I was working with a leader who had just taken over at the helm of a medium-size organization. The company had been led by the previous leader for close to twenty years, and although it was doing well in many areas, the executive team was clearly conflict averse. Office politics drained precious energy away from the vision, and team meetings, while efficient, clearly lacked effectiveness and energy.

About the third month into his tenure, the new leader felt he had made enough observations to get an accurate picture of what was going on, and he had gained enough trust relationally to make his move. It was a simple but effective one.

He came to the next executive team meeting and placed a soft, cuddly, gray elephant in the middle of the circle. As everyone came into the room for the meeting, they saw it sitting there, but the leader made no reference to it as he began the meeting. He watched as eyes darted toward the stuffed animal, and then around the room to see who else was noticing this unintroduced visitor. But he kept going, plowing through agenda item after agenda item.

Finally, after a bit of nervous laughter, one of the guys on the team said, "Hey, what's the deal with the elephant?" And there began a discussion about pachyderms, and how this organization had accumulated them with its culture of conflict avoidance. Wisely, the leader started by admitting to the many times he personally had chosen avoidance over direct conversation. He talked about the fears that caused this, and the kind of corrosive culture that such avoidance could create over the years.

He talked about his deep desire to lead differently, and asked for their help. And while this first meeting was not the last they would have on this topic, they spent a long time that day painfully, slowly, and carefully naming some of the elephants they had lived with for years. It was amazing how healing it was just to name them.

They were all clear eyed in their assessment that this would take a long time to overcome; they had gotten so used to operating this way. It's a lot easier to clean up after an elephant when you know where it is.

But that stuffed animal got them started, and got them talking, and got them wanting to be different. They kept that little guy around for years. Every so often, someone in a meeting would announce that they were "doing it again," so out came the elephant from his home on a shelf, and he was plopped right down in the middle of that team. And everyone knew it was time to talk turkey.

Eventually, that elephant was so worn, his stuffing began falling out. By that time, the team was a different team.

Promises

FOR THOSE OF US who are over thirty, part of the reason we are leaders is that we had people in our lives who were committed to our growth. Someone took the time to develop us. Someone—most likely more than one person—played a significant role in recognizing our gifts and potential, sanding off some of our rough edges, offering us challenging tasks, and then walking beside and behind us while we attempted them.

Most leaders can easily name the people who developed them. And while leadership is never as simple as the sum of those who built it into us, I owe a large part of who I am as a leader to Jamie Barr, Stan and Donna Leonard, Judy Burton, Bill Hybels, Nancy Beach, Max DePree, Allen Phipps, Patrick Lencioni, Jeff Gibson, and Amy Hiett.

Now it's our turn to give to others what has been given to us. And that reciprocity in development grows us as well. It's good for the soul.

Sometimes the critical work of leadership development gets lost in the clamor of the urgent, the crisis of the day, or the fuzziness of exactly how to do it. I hope this chapter will provide a sort of "forced focus" for you on this very important topic.

Leadership development requires open eyes. Open eyes to see those in whom God has deposited the leadership gift.

So what are we looking for? Andy Stanley once said that leaders always think they can do a better job than you are doing. So for starters, we are looking for someone like that. In a situation that might initially make us feel threatened or defensive, we allow the "aha" moments to occur. We never know when we might find a leader in the rough right in front of us—a shepherd in the field.

We need to keep our eyes open for leadership qualities: energy, dissatisfaction, new ideas, mistakes, and perhaps even a bit of cynicism. These are the raw materials in the making of a leader, not the finished product. Leadership development does not necessarily start with strong leadership qualities like discipleship, maturity, and wisdom. Those are the end products. We need to be looking for the drive without the experience, the vision before the patience, the energy minus the discipline. These are the building blocks, the clues that tell us there is a leader here, but so much still needs to be done.

Once, someone saw that in you. Now it's your turn.

Leaders have the best chance to flourish and grow when they are given opportunity, challenge, and relationship. These are the gifts you give to the young leaders in your organizations.

The promises that you make.

The promises that you keep.

Opportunity. An underutilized leader is not a pretty sight. God has wired leaders with ideas, energy, vision, and direction. But when a leader is unable to express these things, frustration and ineffectiveness are often the result. While there is a lot to be said for leaders—especially young ones— proving their character and commitment by filling an open spot, the best move will be to eventually line that leader up with responsibilities that are appropriate to his or her character, experience, and giftedness. And while character

> Once, someone saw that in you. Now it's your turn.

is *always* more important than giftedness, for the most part it ought to be a "both/and" situation. . . . You shouldn't have to choose. You have to work on both.

Leaders need the opportunity to contribute what they do best. Organizations and churches need leaders to do that as well. Giving leaders these opportunities communicates the confidence young leaders need to grow into their giftedness and character.

I was nineteen years old when Jamie Barr gave me significant leadership and teaching roles within the high school ministry at our church. I was twenty-two years old when the hospital I worked at put me in charge of the med-surg wing on the third floor, east side. How old were you? Who invited you in, and to what?

I was underqualified and inexperienced when I was asked to be a teaching pastor and to lead two significant ministries in our last church. But along with those opportunities, I was given direction, coaching, follow-up, coaching, encouragement, and some more coaching. I grew into those roles. Leaders cannot become leaders without significant opportunities.

When I asked to "throw my hat into the ring" for the director position at Axis, I was told that I was not who they were looking for. "In fact," someone said, "you would position about number seventeen on a list of sixteen other candidates we are looking at. You would most definitely not make the final cut of three."

(Did I mention that the encouragement I received did not come until *after* I was named the leader of Axis?)

So, ten months and a nationwide search later, I got the job. Suddenly I was in charge of a large department that had been through some considerable difficulties. It was a complex responsibility, given its mission to make the church relevant to a generation who didn't grow up in church, as well as the fact that we focused on multiple areas: weekend services, worship, preaching, home groups, leadership, volunteers, serving, and events, to name a few.

It was an in-over-my-head, can't-sleep-at-night opportunity. And I had never been happier.

Recently, our firm worked with a large organization that was looking to replace a vice president who had left after serving well for many years. This role was critical to the future of the organization and really needed to be filled with the right person (we should take every position that seriously). So the president and the board acquired the services of a headhunter company and put together a description of the perfect candidate. Many phone calls, e-mails, and meetings later, they had narrowed their search down to two stellar candidates.

During this time, "Bob," one of the underlings of the

exiting vice president, raised his hand and said, "What about me?" He requested that he be considered to take his boss's position. Now things were a bit awkward because no one had even thought about putting this guy's name on the list. He was a great person and a good worker, but he did not even begin to approach the level of his boss.

His request for consideration was politely declined.

He waited a few weeks, and then he asked again. What do you say after you have used the word *awkward*? The thesaurus says "tricky; uncomfortable; embarrassed." Yes, okay, those work.

Again, he was politely told no.

And then something amazing happened. Quietly, while the headhunters, the board, and the president were busy with interviews, Bob just started earning the opportunity. He began to lead like crazy. He realized that although his boss had been terrific, living in his shadow had really stunted his own growth. He had held back and kept from growing and doing the things he *knew* he was capable of doing.

Looking back later, Bob says that he wasn't really looking to prove anything. But he knew deep down that he had not been taking risks or leading as well as he thought he could. He knew there was an opportunity right in front of him that he wanted very much. An in-over-his-head, can't-sleep-at-night opportunity.

And when the president and the board enthusiastically offered him the position, Bob said yes.

Bob's never been happier. He's kicking butt, too.

Challenge. Perhaps more than for most people, challenge is the fuel that leaders run on. A steep learning curve, a major problem, a relational issue that needs a solution—all are necessary fodder for a leader to grow. An appropriate level of challenge spurs the growth of a leader's gift without stretching him or her too far toward the breaking point.

When I took over the leadership of Axis, the staff was *not* glad to see me. Growth had stalled and some of our key volunteer leaders were either leaving or majorly disgruntled. They had weathered more than a year of problems, as well as transitional and temporary leadership.

I had to learn about a generation to which I did not belong. I had to learn to lead people much younger than I was—staff, interns, and volunteers. I had to learn to lead up

Challenge is the fuel that leaders run on.

and sideways in a large organization, since my role in Axis put me on a leadership team that was responsible for all of the adult ministries. I had to learn to lead a team of creative, artistic folks *and* operational, tactical people (that right there may have been one of my biggest and most ongoing challenges). I had to increase my ability to do leadership development across the ministry as well as prompt growth in our attendance, both at the weekend services and in our home groups.

And, at least for the first year, I had to preach almost every week.

I loved the learning and openness and curiosity that my job required. That and the amazing and beloved people I got to do it with. We embraced the challenge together and became students of everything and anything we could get our hands on that would help us do what we were called to do.

We talked to people who knew a lot more about all of this than we did. We invited them out for coffee, and we asked lots of questions. Then we listened. We engaged each other as a staff, talking about what we were learning and how that might make a difference to the organization we were leading.

We embraced new ideas and we considered old ideas. We read books. We visited other ministries doing similar work, and we watched and asked and listened. We prayed and planned, we planned and prayed.

We were open to hearing from others when we made mistakes. We tried to be humble students and confident leaders. We felt energized by the challenge, not discouraged or defeated. This challenge produced an optimism that was infectious.

We kept doing what was working, and we reinvented ourselves when we needed to. We created, maintained, and grew. Together, we determined that obstacles would be times for reflection, dissection, and learning.

We prayed and planned, we planned and prayed.

The organizational and personal challenges we faced were inexorably linked, wed together in that intersection of task and relationship that is so much at the heart of what it means to lead and to be a team.

When you see someone for whom challenge is energizing, you just might have a leader on your hands.

Not long ago, our firm worked with a church leader who was sensing the wrong amount of tension in his own life. He described his situation as being "overworked and underchallenged." We needed to do some shifting of his role that moved him away from busywork outside of his area of giftedness and more toward the kind of leadership work that would leave him excited, exhilarated, and a little overwhelmed. A nice combination for a leader.

Relationship. Leadership is a relationally intensive endeavor. The most effective leaders know that within the context of relationship, the critical issues of authenticity, character, and trust find their voice.

Many leaders make the mistake of ignoring the

relationship, focusing instead on systems and data. No argument, those linear issues of leadership are very important. But they are not the most important. It is easy to lean into those things because they tend to be cut-and-dried and measurable, and they rarely argue back. They are not nearly as time consuming or messy as the relational component of leadership. Perhaps that's also why they are not as important. Even systems and data ultimately have to be put in the context of people.

And a relationship should not be seen as simply a "leadership strategy." Great leaders focus on the relational part of leadership because they want to. They may not want to all the time, but mostly, they want to. Great leaders like and enjoy people.

The best leaders I worked for knew me. They weren't my best friends. I didn't want or expect that, but I did want them to know me. Some of our interactions began with business issues, but others began with a question regarding something going on in my life. Never inappropriate, but always interested.

Great leaders like and enjoy people.

Quite a few years ago, I was on an international trip with some colleagues, including my boss. Somewhere in Switzerland the conversation turned to one guy's middle name. These are the kind of inane conversations you can get involved in when jet lag and work collide. Anyway, in response to the conversation, I expressed my surprise that our boss didn't know this guy's middle name.

To which he replied, "Why would I?"

"Oh, I don't know," I said. "I would just guess after fifteen plus years of working together, the topic might have come up."

Shrug. A look of confusion, change of topic, and then we moved on.

Until dinner that night. The guy we'd been talking about leaned over and said to me, "I've always liked my job, but him not knowing my middle name? He doesn't know anything about me."

Now, I trust you know that I am not saying you need to learn everyone's middle name. But I do think this example is a good picture of a leadership dynamic that hurt rather than helped. A genuine concern for and knowledge of those you work with is fundamental to great leadership.

In the work I currently do, my partners and I often have the opportunity to sit down with leaders of businesses, superintendents of school districts, directors of nonprofit organizations, and pastors of churches. Almost always, our conversations include a discussion of the people on their leadership team. Time and time again, we've found that those who exhibit the strongest leadership give a great "color commentary" when asked about their team. In addition to describing what the people on their teams do, these leaders also share stories about their families, friends, and personal lives. They know the people on their teams, their histories, their current interests, and their kids' ages.

Strong relationships create the context in which good opportunities and appropriate challenges can be distributed. Trust is cultivated within relationships, and we all know what great things can happen on a team and in an organization when trust is present.

Good relationships add that extra punch that keeps the best and brightest wanting to work in your organization. Relationships reflexively create collaboration rather than hierarchy, trust rather than suspicion, and joy rather than drudgery. If you can provide a place for people to work where they can do what they do best and do it with people they like, you've created a dynamic combination.

Rubber Bands III

STRETCHING PEOPLE INCLUDES involving them in the process. Helping someone find his or her best fit is an interactive endeavor that incorporates your observations of who they are along with their own take on those observations. When I first arrived at Willow Creek, one of the senior leaders spent more than an hour with me in his office. He asked me question after question, all around the issue of what I enjoyed doing and what I was good at.

Conversations like this are incredibly powerful. Think about the last few years of your life. How many times has someone engaged you in a conversation that was directed solely toward understanding who you are and what you do well? You don't need many of them, but when they happen they can be very clarifying and directive. As a leader, you need to be initiating them on a regular basis with the people in your organization.

In Axis, I needed to do this with staff, interns, volunteers, and regular attendees. So I developed a very simple flow to help me: Ask-Observe-Place-Adjust.

Ask. This part was easy. I started with simple questions: Tell me what kinds of things you really love doing. What brings you energy? What topics would keep you engaged in a conversation to the point that you might lose track of the time? What experiences have you had, on a job or outside of that realm, where you have done something and done it well? What kinds of things drain your energy? What parts of your current job do you avoid or procrastinate, either because you aren't good at them or because you simply don't enjoy doing them?

When a leader initiates this kind of a conversation, people feel honored and paid attention to. It keeps a leader's focus on the people, and not just on the programs and the systems.

Whenever I talk to people about what they enjoy doing and what they are good at, it helps me to make better decisions when it comes to placing them in an area within an organization that lines up with those passions.

But for some people, answers to these questions don't come easy. If those you are leading are young, lack experience, or have simply never given much thought to these types of questions, the best thing you can do is to encourage them with the word *try*. Ask them to choose a role, project, or ministry that seems intriguing, and then *try* it for six months or a year.

I always encourage people to make a six-months-to-a-year commitment, both for themselves as well as for the area that is taking them in. It often takes people that long to really live deeply in the experience before they can determine if it is a fit. And if an area of the organization is willing to take a risk on someone without experience, the people involved in that area deserve enough time to benefit from their investment.

Observe. Once I ask people to share what they most enjoy, I then spend some time talking about what *I* have seen in them: areas of giftedness, skill, and passion. You can also gather feedback from other leaders and those they work with. These observations from outside eyes help them—and you—to get a better view of their effectiveness and fit, along with ways in which they can grow.

When I first started working for Axis, a young man named Brad emerged with much enthusiasm for leadership. But from what I had observed, although he was a gifted leader, he had spent much of the past year jumping from area to area, changing whenever it got difficult or he got bored.

It is tempting, when you don't have many leaders, to say "good enough" too quickly. And while it is true you can't wait for perfect leaders, I had concerns about Brad's ability to persevere and commit to something.

One afternoon, Brad came to me bubbling with excitement over a new group we were starting. He wanted to be a part of the new endeavor and couldn't wait to get started. I said, "How about if you continue to lead where you are right now, and let's see where things are in six months?" I could tell he did not like my response, which interestingly made me all the more committed to that direction. I knew that if Brad continued jumping around to different areas of leadership, he could easily end up harming the ministry more than helping it.

In addition, and probably more importantly, Brad would hurt himself. Something unhealthy was driving this constant movement. My responsibility as a leader was both to the ministry and to Brad.

So Brad, not happily, moved back to his area and stayed for the next six months. And I watched him out of the corner of my eye. In fact, to be perfectly honest, I kind of ignored Brad on purpose. I had gotten the sense that much of what drove his leadership was the need to be noticed and applauded.

You have probably already made the connection, but my strong suspicion was that I was able to recognize all these things about Brad because, well, you know . . .

After about seven months, I invited Brad out to lunch. We had a great conversation. I mean *great*. I wish you could have been there. We moved rapidly to bedrock issues of pride and insecurity (funny how they almost always pop up together), of his frustration with me, and of his need for approval and attention.

He spoke about how, just a couple of months into the process, God had shown him these things. He had realized that leading was not fundamentally about him. Of course it was in some ways, but in other ways he had not noticed before, it was about others. And once he made this connection, he began to really love the people he was responsible for. He found himself leading and leading well, not noticing if anyone else was noticing.

He knew the names and stories of everyone on his team. He knew their strengths and weaknesses. He had aligned them on the team accordingly and was a great encourager of their efforts. He directed their actions and spoke honestly to them when he saw sin in their lives. He assisted them when they needed support, he built trust with them, and he shared from his heart about who God was and why they were doing what they were doing.

Sometimes six months can make all the difference in the world. Brad had a couple of people on his team that he had readied to take over his leadership, and when he moved on, that team kept going with barely a hiccup.

Leadership is a relationally intensive job.

And we did move Brad on. We put him in a leadership role on another team that he was so excited about. For the next few years, Brad led that team to flourishing. The multiple teams he oversaw were full—actually some had a waiting list of people wanting to join. The area he led was full of life and people were transformed as a result. Brad was too.

Place/Adjust. After the asking and observing is done, I begin to place people in an area that lines up with their gifts. And then, by continuing the conversation, I know when and where I need to make adjustments to that placement. Sometimes adjustments are made in terms of support to make their placement work. Sometimes it means a slight move or additional skills training.

One of the most important aspects of this phase is the continued engagement of you as the leader. Did I mention that leadership is a relationally intensive job? The success of a person's placement is dependent on your keeping your eyes on the situation, along with ongoing discussion. It is critical that you continue interacting both with the person who has been placed and those who are working with that person in that role.

This part of the process can be frustrating and discouraging for everyone involved. Sometimes you have to have those difficult but necessary conversations—with people who view themselves as teachers but find they cannot teach, with people in administrative roles who have trouble organizing. But between the perseverance required to keep going and the humility to sometimes hear the painful truth, you can help those you lead to find the right spot. And once you do, it will be worth all the effort.

"So, what do you love to do?"

One of the most gratifying moments I have ever had as a leader was the day that I overheard a conversation between Brad and one of his volunteers: "So, what do you love to do?"

understatement *of the Year*

A COUPLE OF MONTHS AGO I was getting ready to leave to speak at a leadership conference. The organizers had given me a topic to speak about when they had booked me, and I was just putting the notes for that talk in my briefcase and getting ready to head to the airport, when someone from the conference called.

They had been thinking and wondered if I could do a talk on something else instead. Apparently one of the speakers hadn't been given an assignment ahead of time, and just that very day had spoken on my subject.

Really? You mean I will have the *entire* plane ride to decide on a topic and write a whole new talk? Really, you shouldn't have.

So as the plane was taxiing down the runway, I cracked open a stack of blank paper and began. For some reason, pages of blank, white paper help me do some of my best thinking.

I began to think about what leaders need to hear, and the kinds of things that keep them from being all they need to be. After mulling over all these thoughts for a while, I wrote a talk entitled "Stop Being Surprised That Leadership Is Hard."

We waste an awful lot of time as leaders being continually surprised at the difficulties we face. I think it simply helps to know that you are exactly right. It *is* stinking hard, and once you know that and can remind yourself of it every time, you can move much more quickly past the surprise of it and get on with the work of leading.

I began to think back on the many question-and-answer sessions I had ever been a part of, either as a speaker or a participant. Of all the questions that get asked, most often the person needs to hear not only what to do in a difficult situation, but also just some confirmation that what he or she is facing is tough.

We've all heard the terrific tenet that says when you find what you are gifted to do, do that. One of the unspoken nuances of that principle is that there is a big difference between being good at something and that something being easy. My husband is good at golf, but he would never say it is easy. He is also good at preaching sermons, but I have never observed it to be an easy process for him, especially the hard work of researching and crafting those talks. He is good at writing, but watching him agonize over those pages put me at fifty-two years old before I ever decided to write a book of my own.

Something that you're good at and something that is easy—worlds apart. But the combination of "good at" and "hard work" is amazingly satisfying.

Yes, it's true. As a leader, you may have signed on for one of the toughest jobs. You are not wrong. Okay, next question.

Leadership is already difficult, and in this moment in time we must add the complexities of the collision of modern and postmodern cultures, the familiar but accelerated issue of rate of change, and the emerging global village that is reshaping reality. A leader without courage, resilience, optimism, curiosity, and perseverance will simply not last.

> **The combination of "good at" and "hard work" is amazingly satisfying.**

This is not about getting paid more to keep you in the game. This is about being a completely different—and better—kind of leader.

Not only is the old model of the omnicompetent leader dated, it simply won't work anymore. There is too much to accomplish for one person to be responsible for or capable of handling everything. Too much is at stake and the world is moving too quickly for us to go back. People want to be a part of something together, not just following the leader.

Late one evening when I was an emergency room nurse, a confused and frantic babysitter rushed through our automatic glass doors. In her arms, she carried a limp, barely conscious three-year-old boy wrapped in a blanket. She had been taking care of him for two nights while his parents were out of town on a short vacation.

The illness had come on suddenly, with a slight cough giving way to a fever over 104 degrees and a rapidly increasing lethargy. She was absolutely beside herself as we whisked that child onto a gurney and into a treatment room.

People want to be a part of something together, not just following the leader.

Immediately a team of highly trained, passionate people sprang into action under the leadership of a gifted emergency room physician.

And of all the options that doctor had at his disposal, the one thing he didn't have was the ability to save that kid by himself. Time was too precious, there was too much at stake, and too many things needed to be done for one person to accomplish everything. There was no other option except for that team of people, functioning as peers, to be well led by one.

In what looked like a choreographed event, the doctor quickly assessed the kid's condition and effortlessly slipped a breathing tube in his airway, all the while calling out for one person to set up a spinal tap tray, the X-ray technician to get a portable chest film, the lab person to draw blood and send it for immediate tests and results. He asked the nurse to insert a catheter and check vital signs, and called out a series of medications to be administered as soon as the IV was in. He responded to test results by asking for oxygen to be started, and made changes in the medications as new information came in.

Test results, along with a telltale rash, confirmed our worst fear: bacterial meningitis. At one point, about forty minutes into our efforts, the doctor paused for just a moment as the seriousness of the situation began to set in. He looked us all in the eyes and said, "We need to save this kid." And without another word, something clicked, and we all moved into an even higher level of precision, flow, and determination.

Later, as we all stood around and talked about the

experience, the doctor admitted that he had added thinking like a parent into the matrix of thinking like a doctor and thinking like a leader. During those first forty minutes of working on that child, the doctor knew that the nurse at the front desk was calling the parents, who would surely ask questions in fear and disbelief, and then get into a car for the two-hour drive home—while we were simultaneously trying to save their child.

He said that in medical school, most of the teachers talked about separating personal feelings from the work. Made sense. Until one teacher told them just the opposite. Outside of the obvious need for boundaries and separation, this teacher told them they would be much better leaders in the world of medicine if they factored in the relational component of treatment. The doctor we worked with that night said that perspective changed everything for him.

There were a couple of times that night when the boy quickly deteriorated, and each time there was the intense, focused, quiet work of a determined team, with the background noise of machines and procedures. Things got so bad at one point that even though the parents had arrived, the doctor couldn't leave the room to talk with them.

You could have cut the tension in that room with a knife. We all wanted him to be able to go out and tell those parents that their boy would make it.

A few hours later, he did. And he did.

There is simply too much at stake, and things are simply moving too quickly for us to do anything but build and lead a *great* team of people. Get people who are better than you and be glad for it. Get people who can come up with new and innovative ways to do things, and applaud that. Get people who will tell you the truth and make great, collaborative decisions. Get people who will relentlessly pursue the best, both for themselves and for everyone in the organization. Get strong leaders at every level in the organization.

Get strong leaders at every level in the organization.

Get them and then lead them. Lead them at the level they deserve to be led, which will demand more from you than ever before. Yes, this kind of leadership is hard. Yes, this kind of leadership is great.

Leadership is hard because it requires clarity. And if clarity isn't hard, it isn't clarity. It can be simple, but it cannot be easy.

Leaders are obligated to tell people what is expected of them. If they don't, people will move toward what is urgent or what is easy. Neither of which may be their best contribution to the organization.

Here's what I mean. If I go to work for you every day

and you have not told me what you expect me to do, I am operating in a vacuum, and with a fair amount of anxiety. I am not by nature an anxious person. I just don't have any idea what I should be spending the majority of my time on. So when someone else presents something as urgent, or if *nothing* presents itself as urgent, I start looking around for file cabinets that need cleaning out. At least I will know when that job is done. Well, there I go. Spending all of my well-intended energy on someone else's agenda.

And then, through no fault of my own, the organization is not driven by the vision, but by everyone else's sense of what is important at any given moment, or by the myriad of easy jobs at my fingertips. Talk about a diffusion of energy, and a loss of vision.

I don't think I like working for you.

And then I sense your mounting frustration that what is supposed to be getting done isn't. But since you haven't been direct with me about what I should be spending my time on, why should I expect you to be direct about your frustration? And so, in the way that only passive-aggressive responses can produce, I have this vague and uneasy sense that you are not happy with me even though you never say anything. Not with words anyway. But you sure communicate displeasure indirectly. Not many things more miserable than enduring that.

No, I am *sure* I don't like working for you, and a guy down in accounting has a brother-in-law who just started a landscaping business, and they need a telemarketer. So in goes my two week's notice, and you are left believing that you just can't get good workers these days.

Leaders owe clarity, both to the organization and to the individuals at every level.

Leadership is hard.

I just want to repeat that a couple of times in this chapter so you don't miss it.

Leadership matters. It matters deeply. It matters that we live out our lives in the giftedness that God graciously bestowed, and that we help others do the same. Much of that is at the heart of what it means to lead.

It's important that what we do intersects with what the world needs, that the work we do has a favorable and strong impact on this beautiful and broken world. God's beautiful and broken world.

Leadership matters. It stands at the crossroads of what we do and who we are, and that is a profound place. It requires that we shape vision and develop a plan and work hard. It requires that we become stronger in our resilience and forgiveness and determination and love.

Profound places bring with them requirements and obligations, and leadership is no exception. Even when we would rather wait until the problems come to us before we respond, leadership requires that we go looking for and initiate and move toward the problems so that we can intercept them when they are small.

As leaders, we are obliged to expand our capacity for chaos and change, and increase our tolerance for necessary ambiguity. We are obliged to add to that the discipline and structure needed at the right moment in order to solidify and direct everyone's efforts.

We owe to those we lead a level of communication that goes beyond saying things once, and we owe them the time and creativity to make those communications clear and reasonable and compelling. The grace of our words, the urgency that synergizes, and the repetition that reminds— these things are our responsibility.

Leaders bear the burden of leadership. Not so much that others have nothing to do, but enough so that the burden doesn't become a discouragement to those on the team. Leaders bear the burden so that hope has free reign. We do not carry the burden out of ego, but rather out of hope.

Perhaps the greatest enemy of leadership is discouragement. And if that's the case, one of the best treatments is knowing that leadership is hard. Perhaps that knowledge will keep discouragement at bay enough to allow you the space to grow into the leadership needed to move forward.

Some discouragement is our own fault. The results of poor leadership *ought* to be discouraging. When our stubbornness, our pride, our lack of knowledge, or so many other possibilities create discouragement, the results are deserved. And it ought to be a prompt for apologies, correction, and growth.

But much of the discouragement that saps the energy from leaders is inevitable. And sometimes that discouragement is wearying to the point that we want to give up, or worse, we decide to stay but end up leading in mediocre ways.

Leadership is hard, and we all need to stop being surprised by that. We need to give it a slight chuckle and a nod, and then keep going.

Because leadership matters. Done well, it is one of the most rewarding endeavors there is. And it matters wherever it is done. It might seem like it only matters at Microsoft or Apple. But it doesn't. It matters at companies whose names you wouldn't even recognize. You might think it only matters at McKesson or Cleveland University Hospital, but it also matters at small pharmaceutical companies that aren't traded on NASDAQ, and at small community hospitals that serve generations of the same families.

You'd think great leadership only matters at famous non-profit organizations like Make-A-Wish or the Leukemia/

Lymphoma Society, but it also matters at small, unknown groups that are feeding the poor and housing the homeless and raising money to support public education. It matters as much at these places as it does anywhere else.

For every Zagat-rated restaurant, there's a mom-and-pop eatery that's being well led. For every large university, there's a local junior college that is being led by great leaders. For every megachurch that has its own leadership conference, there is a small or medium-size church that's getting it right. It doesn't have to be famous to be great.

It is so easy to mistake well known for better, and renown for expert. It isn't so. And since most of us lead out of the spotlight, we need to remind ourselves that leadership right where we are is desperately important. Being in the top 1 percent is much too narrow a place to call success. Don't wait to get famous to get good.

Your best leadership efforts are needed on a daily basis, right where you are.

So whatever that takes, do it. Get out the rubber bands, the books, and the Post-it notes. Stretch them, read them, post them. And start by convincing yourself that leadership matters.

Faith is a vision that our destiny is to be absorbed
in a tremendously creative team effort,
with unimaginably splendid leadership,
on an inconceivably vast plane of activity,
with ever more comprehensive cycles of productivity and enjoyment—
and that is what eye has not seen, nor ear heard,
that was before us in the prophetic vision.

DALLAS WILLARD

About the Author

Nancy Ortberg is a founding partner of Teamworx2, a business and leadership consulting firm that provides fast-paced, practical, and compelling sessions to leaders and their teams. Teamworx2 works with businesses, schools, nonprofits, and churches to address issues of organizational effectiveness and teamwork.

A former teaching pastor at Willow Creek Community Church, Nancy has spoken at the Stanford University Graduate School of Business, Catalyst, the Leadership Forum, the Telecare Leadership Conference, the Omnicell Leadership Conference, the Rethink Conference, and the Orange conference. She is also a consulting partner for Patrick Lencioni, president of the Table Group and best-selling author of *The Five Dysfunctions of a Team*.

Nancy and her husband, John, live in the Bay Area and have three children, Laura, Mallory, and Johnny.

Acknowledgments

Collective efforts always yield something more magnificent than those made by a single person. This book is no exception, and is much better for the fingerprints of Carol, Kathy, Lisa, Elizabeth, Ron, and Jennifer at Tyndale House Publishers. I am grateful for your belief, encouragement, and vast efforts.

To the many, many wonderful mentors in leadership I have had over the years. To Jamie Barr, Max DePree, Barbara Harrison, Bill Hybels, Nancy Beach, Dick Anderson, Russ Robinson, Patrick Lencioni, Amy Hiett, Jeff Gibson, and David Simpson, to name a few—I am daily and eternally grateful.

And to John, Laura, Mallory, and Johnny, who inspire and delight me on a regular basis.

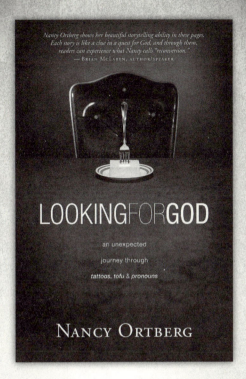

Nancy Ortberg shows her beautiful storytelling ability in these pages.
Each story is like a clue in a quest for God, and through them,
readers can experience what Nancy calls "reconversion."
— BRIAN MCLAREN, AUTHOR/SPEAKER

LOOKINGFORGOD

an unexpected

journey through

tattoos, tofu & pronouns

NANCY ORTBERG

In her long-awaited debut title, Nancy Ortberg will inspire you to break away from the bland, formulaic approach to Christianity and embrace the often unexpected, at times unnerving, but always extraordinary power of God's grace. As you journey with Nancy, you'll come to discover God in places you would have never dreamed of looking, and you'll experience faith on a deeper level than you ever imagined possible!

> "Whether you're a theologian, a regular churchgoer, a nominal Christian, or just curious about this Jesus guy everyone is talking about, *Looking for God* will overwhelm you. It is remarkably profound, poignant, and insightful, and written with an uncommon and inspired sense of joy."
>
> **PATRICK LENCIONI**, best-selling author of
> *The Five Dysfunctions of a Team*